Frank Lorenz

Basics of Phonetics & English Phonology

with IPA Transcription

Grafische Elemente Einband
© Petr Vaclavek, Daniel Ernst / Fotolia.com

Abbildungen 1,2,3,4,6 und Einbandgestaltung
André Luttermann

Abbildung 12 und Tabelle 16
© 2005 International Phonetic Association
http://www.langsci.ucl.ac.uk/ipa/ipachart.html

Bibliografische Information der Deutschen Nationalbibliothek

Die Deutsche Nationalbibliothek verzeichnet diese Publikation in der
Deutschen Nationalbibliografie; detaillierte bibliografische Daten sind
im Internet über http://dnb.d-nb.de abrufbar.

ISBN 978-3-8325-3109-6

Logos Verlag Berlin GmbH
Comeniushof, Gubener Str. 47,
10243 Berlin
Tel.: +49 (0)30 42 85 10 90
Fax: +49 (0)30 42 85 10 92
INTERNET: http://www.logos-verlag.de

Contents
['kɒntɛnts]

Contents
['kɒntɛnts]

Contents
['kɒntɛnts]

Contents
['kɒntɛnts]

Note to Instructors
[ˈnəʊt tu ɪnˈstrʌktəz]

At many German universities, phonetics is taught as a class in its own right within the curriculum of a BA in English Studies. Often it is taught at a very early stage, in the second, if not first semester. This textbook caters for the needs of these students in that it provides a basic but sound knowledge of phonetics without taking any knowledge of other linguistic disciplines for granted.

This book is structured in twelve chapters that students can follow throughout a phonetics course. In parallel, transcription exercises are included with each chapter in order to train students in IPA transcription practice.

The book diverges from many other textbooks on phonetics in the following points:

Phonetics and Pronunciation: Many textbooks focus solely on phonetics and phonology, leaving pronunciation tips and transcription aside. Other works focus only on improving students' pronunciation skills, without any phonetic theory. This work aims at encompassing both.

Phonemes and allophones: While the importance to differentiate between letters and sounds is pointed out from the start, the difference between phonemes and allophones has been postponed to a later chapter, when students are able to see the richness of allophonic variation and comprehend the concept better.

Consonants and vowels: The articulation of consonants and vowels is described in general, also giving examples from other languages.

Weak forms: Weak forms of function words are introduced early together with vowels, so that students may use these in transcription right from the start.

Acoustic phonetics: The book includes a basic chapter on acoustic phonetics, which is missing in many textbooks.

Syllabification: The book contains a chapter on syllable structure. Although not all criteria relevant for syllabification can be included, sonority, the

7

maximum onset principle, phonotactic onset constraints and the status of checked vowels are explained.

Suprasegmentals: While many textbooks use transcription at first, but revert to orthographic spelling when turning to word stress and intonation, transcription is used throughout in this book.

Transcription standard: All transcriptions are both in Received Pronunciation and General American. The main differences between these two standards are also explained. In a few tables, where the segmental level was not the point of illustration, General American has be omitted for reasons of legibility.

Dress vowel: The sounds in (dress) and (square) are transcribed as [ɛ] and [ɛə̯]. Traditionally, the vowel has been claimed to be in-between cardinal vowels [e] and [ɛ], when in fact it is much closer (if not identical) to cardinal [ɛ]. (e.g. Deterding 1997 on formants of English monophthongs). Even though many dictionaries transcribe this sound as [e] for reasons of simplicity, this confuses students who also learn German transcription or work on regional accents of English. Therefore, correctness has been given preference over simplicity.

Diphthongs: The second part of a diphthong is marked with the symbol for non-syllabic in order to differentiate it from two monophthongs in sequence. The FACE diphthong is transcribed as [eɪ̯], as its starting point is higher than the DRESS vowel and in accents where it becomes monophthongised it is [feːs] not [fɛːs]. Triphthongs are considered to be non-existent in English. Words such as (fire) or (hour) are either spoken with a diphthong plus schwa or if they are indeed monosyllabic, it is much more likely that they are pronounced with a diphthong such as [faə̯].

1 Phonetics, Phonology, Transcription
[fəˈnɛtɪks | fəˈnɒlədʒi | trænˈskrɪpʃn̩]

Phonetics vs. Phonology

Phonetics and Phonology are two sister sciences that investigate speech sounds. Although both share the main subject of oral human communication, they differ very much in their approach. While phonetics is interested in the speaking process as such, phonology is more concerned with its contribution to the system of a language.

Phonetics overlaps with other natural sciences like biology, physics or medicine. In the production of speech sounds, it investigates the organs that are involved in the speech process, their anatomy and how they function. Phonetics is interested in speech sounds as such and their acoustic properties. A growing number of technological devices and applications employ speech recognition and speech synthesis systems: users give voice commands to their mobile phone when driving or want a written text to be read back to them. This raises the question of what can be measured in a speech sound and how the vowels and consonants of human language differ from each other physically. Furthermore, phonetics is interested in how the brain works and what processes are running when we speak and listen to language.

Phonology, on the other hand, is, like linguistics, more interested in the language system and the rules by which it is governed. Language uses a vast number of sounds, all of which phonetics can describe. Phonology sorts through these and asks which of them play a role in communication. Taking the German word ⟨reich⟩ as an example, if one substitutes the sound represented by ⟨ch⟩ with ⟨f⟩, it becomes a different word. If it is substituted with the consonant sound heard in ⟨ach⟩, on the other hand, it sounds like a Swiss accent, but it is essentially still the same word. Furthermore, phonology seeks to find out which sounds can be combined into words. Although there are many words in English that start with [bl] or [gl], there is none that starts with [dl]. While speech sounds and their combinations constitute the segmental level, suprasegmental phonology examines information that is communicated in addition to that, for instance the speech melody of a sentence signalling whether an utterance is a statement or a question.

As both phonetics and phonology have spoken language as their subject, both need a way of representing this medium in some way. That ordinary writing is not sufficient, but a different transcription system is needed, becomes apparent when looking at the relationship between letters and sounds.

Letters and Sounds

Written words stand for spoken ones and any spoken word can be written down. However, there is no one-to-one relationship between a written letter and a spoken sound. In linguistics, letters are put in angle brackets ⟨ ⟩ and sounds in square brackets [ ].

A combination of two letters can stand for one sound, as for instance the digraph ⟨sh⟩ that corresponds to one sound only, transcribed as [ʃ]. The same sound is represented in German by a combination of three letters: ⟨sch⟩. In French, by the two letters ⟨ch⟩.

Other sounds do not have a direct letter correspondence at all. The sound [ʤ], for example, is represented by ⟨j⟩ in ⟨joke⟩, by ⟨g⟩ in ⟨gin⟩ and by ⟨dg⟩ in ⟨judge⟩. Normally, however, these letters have a different corresponding sound that can be heard in the words ⟨year⟩ and ⟨go⟩, for instance.

In English, the gap between the spelling of a word and its pronunciation is particularly wide. The main reason is that English has a traditional or historic spelling: the spelling is still the same as several hundred years ago, although the pronunciation has changed considerably in the meantime.

The same combination of letters can be pronounced in a variety of ways and the only possibility to pronounce a word correctly is to know its pronunciation.

cough	tough	bough	through	though	thoroughfare
⟨ough⟩					
[ɒf]	[ʌf]	[aʊ̯]	[uː]	[əʊ̯]	[ə]

Table 1: letter-to-sound correspondences, reproduced from Finegan (2007)

Conversely, for the same sound sequence countless different spellings can be found.

see	senile	sea	seize	scenic	siege	ceiling	cedar	cease	juicy	glossy
see	se	sea	sei	sce	sie	cei	ce	cea	cy	sy
[siː]										

Table 2: sound-to-letter correspondences, reproduced from Finegan (2007)

When dealing with spoken language, a system is therefore needed that is able to transcribe language as it is spoken in an unambiguous way.

IPA – International Phonetics Alphabet

The International Phonetics Alphabet, short IPA (sometimes also API from its French name *alphabet phonétique international*) is a set of transcription symbols that is used by linguists and phoneticians to transcribe spoken language.

In IPA, one symbol corresponds to exactly one sound. While in standard spelling there is no one-to-one correspondence between letters and sounds, this rule is paramount in IPA. The reverse is also true that one sound is always transcribed with the same symbol.

As the name suggests, the IPA is not limited to one language, but it is international. The IPA allows transcription of any sounds humans are capable of producing for the sake of speaking. Thus, with the set of symbols provided by the IPA, any language can be transcribed.

Although IPA transcription may look exotic at first, it is actually quite accessible since another principle of the IPA is that of simplicity. Wherever possible, the IPA uses standard roman letters. So the phonetic symbol for the sound represented by ⟨p⟩ in most languages is in fact [p] in IPA. Because there are more sounds than the Latin alphabet provides letters for, other symbols, variations of existing letters (e.g. upside-down [ə]) or letters from other alphabets (e.g. [θ] from the Greek alphabet) are also employed.

11

Standards of English Pronunciation

Received Pronunciation

The standard pronunciation of British English is Received Pronunciation ("received" in the sense of generally accepted), short RP. Received Pronunciation is sometimes also called BBC English or the Queen's English, which shows the impact these two institutions have had on it.

Received Pronunciation is a non-local accent. Traditionally it was spoken by educated people who had attended one of the prestigious boarding schools and the universities of Oxford or Cambridge. With the foundation of BBC radio in 1922, RP received a boost, as the BBC insisted on its use by newsreaders. Thus, the number of people exposed to this accent increased.

It is important to understand that RP, similar to any pronunciation standard, is strictly speaking hardly spoken by anyone, but still serves as a model of pronunciation, which educated people try to approximate.

General American

The US American standard pronunciation is called General American, short GA. This standard accent is also referred to as Network English which, as with RP, demonstrates the huge role the media have played in its making.

Originally, General American developed from Midwestern accents southwest of the Great Lakes, but today it is the most neutral and non-localised accent in the United States. Because GA is not associated with any class, it is in fact estimated to be spoken by a large proportion of the population.

Where GA diverges from RP, the pronunciation is indicated after a double bar (‖). In a few tables, it has been omitted for better legibility.

IPA on Computers

In order to insert IPA transcription symbols on a computer, a unicode font needs to be used that contains these characters. From Windows Vista onwards, the fonts Arial, Courier New, Segoe UI, Tahoma and Times New Roman include IPA symbols. Alternatively, several fonts are available for download free of charge.

Andika	http://scripts.sil.org/Andika_download
Cardo	http://scholarsfonts.net/cardofnt.html
Charis SIL	http://scripts.sil.org/CharisSIL_download
DejaVu	http://dejavu-fonts.org
Doulos SIL	http://scripts.sil.org/DoulosSIL_download
Gentium	http://scripts.sil.org/Gentium_download
Junicode	http://junicode.sourceforge.net

Table 3: fonts containing IPA symbols

For roman letters, the normal keyboard can be used. Additional IPA symbols can be inserted with the Insert/Symbol function in Microsoft Word and other programmes. For more convenient typing, a keyboard driver, the Unicode Phonetic Keyboard, is provided by the University College London at http://www.phon.ucl.ac.uk/resource/phonetics/.

IPA Transcription Symbols

iː	ɪ	ʊ	uː	oʊ GA	eɪ	ɪə RP	ɚ GA
fleece	*kit*	*foot*	*goose*	*goat*	*face*	*near*	*letter*
ɛ	ə	ɜː RP	ɔː	əʊ RP	ɔɪ	ʊə RP	ɜːr GA
dress	*ago*	*nurse*	*thought*	*goat*	*choice*	*cure*	*nurse*
æ	ʌ	ɑː	ɒ RP	aʊ	aɪ	ɛə RP	
trap	*strut*	*palm*	*lot*	*mouth*	*price*	*square*	
p	b	t	d	tʃ	dʒ	k	g
pen	*back*	*tea*	*day*	*church*	*age*	*key*	*get*
f	v	θ	ð	s	z	ʃ	ʒ
fine	*move*	*thing*	*this*	*soon*	*zero*	*ship*	*vision*
m	n	ŋ	h	l	r	w	j
more	*nice*	*long*	*hot*	*light*	*road*	*wet*	*yes*

Table 4: overview of IPA symbols, GA vowels in grey

Transcribe with care!

- ✓ Always put transcriptions in square brackets [ ].
- ✓ If you transcribe a text, put the text in brackets, not individual words.
- ✓ Do not use punctuation or capital letters. A pause can be marked with |.
- ✓ Transcribe numbers or abbreviations as they are spoken.
- ✓ Learn the length sign [ː] together with the IPA symbol.
- ✓ [ɑː] has a script A, while [aʊ] and [aɪ] have a typewriter A.
- ✓ [ə] is an ⟨e⟩ turned on its head. It is not [ɘ]. It is as high as [e].
- ✓ [θ] is the Greek letter theta and as high as [t]. It is not [ө].
- ✓ [ɛ] is an epsilon. In [ɜː] it is flipped and looks like a small three.
- ✓ For [ŋ], the right leg bends inwards. It is not [ɲ] or [ɳ].
- ✓ [o] does not exist in English, except in the GA diphthong [oʊ].

⇒ one symbol = one sound

Exercises

1.1

Decide how many sounds you hear in the following words.

5	_motion_		
6	_DVD_		
4	_money_		

future 4	_measure_ 4	_mission_ 5
dictionary 9	_garage_ 5	_night_ 3
university 9	_fishing_ 5	_eyesight_ 4

1.2

The following words are frequently mispronounced by English language learners. With the help of the IPA table, try to pronounce them correctly. ['] signals that the following syllable is accentuated.

	🇬🇧	🇺🇸
determine	[di'tɜ:mɪn]	[di'tɜ˞:mɪn]
examine	[ɪg'zæmɪn]	
gesture	['ʤɛstʃə]	['ʤɛstʃɚ]
hypothesis	[haɪ'pɒθəsɪs]	[haɪ'pɑ:θəsɪs]
occur	[ə'kɜ:]	[ə'kɜ˞:]
preference	['prɛfrəns]	
salient	['seɪli̯ənt]	
strategy	['strætəʤi]	
variable	['vɛərɪəbl̩]	['vɛrɪəbl̩]
interlocutor	[ɪntə'lɒkjʊtə]	[ɪntɚ'lɑ:kjətɚ]
ambiguity	[æmbɪ'gju:əti]	
anxious	['æŋkʃəs]	
vowel	['vaʊ̯əl]	

Hypo-thesis
occur

15

1.3

Transcribe the following passage from *The Adventures of Tom Sawyer* by Mark Twain, using the IPA table above.

If you find this exercise too difficult, work the other way round and try to read the solution at the end of the book.

Tom appeared on the sidewalk with a bucket of whitewash and a long-handled brush. He surveyed the fence, and all gladness left him and a deep melancholy settled down upon his spirit. Thirty yards of board fence nine feet high. Life to him seemed hollow, and existence but a burden. Sighing, he dipped his brush and passed it along the topmost plank; repeated the operation; did it again; compared the insignificant whitewashed streak with the far-reaching continent of unwhitewashed fence, and sat down on a tree-box discouraged.

Listen to a recording of the transcription text online at:
www.phonetiker.net/transcript/

[tɒm əpɪəd ɒn ðə saɪdwɔːk wɪθ ə bʌkɪt əf waɪtwɒʃ
ənd ə lɒŋ-hændl̩d brʌʃ

2 The Speech Process
[ðə ˈspiːʧ prəʊ̯sɛs]

Spoken language is sound. Sound, in turn, is a fluctuation in air pressure. It is something tangible, which anyone will understand who has ever stood next to a loudspeaker at a festival or in a nightclub. Sound is something real that humans are capable of producing with their bodies. A number of organs are involved in the speech process, before the sound they produce leaves the mouth: the lungs, the pharynx, the oral and nasal cavity. It is interesting to note that speech production is not the primary function of any of these organs: the lungs are responsible for the exchange of oxygen and carbon dioxide, mouth and nose for the ingestion of food. Only in a secondary function do these organs participate in the speech process.

Initiation

In order to produce a fluctuation in air pressure, air is needed as a carrier. Without being physically correct, it could be said that sound is air that has been processed in some way. Without air, there cannot be sound.

For the vast majority of speech sounds, the air coming from the lungs is used. While we exhale, this air is turned into sound. Because it is a continuous airstream flowing outwards from the lungs which is the basis for speech sounds, it is called an egressive pulmonic airstream. All sounds of English are produced with an egressive pulmonic airstream. Languages across the world have other modes of initiation, for instance in click sounds. In English, clicks only occur when speakers tut in disapproval: "tsk tsk" starts with a click, for which no air from the lungs is needed.

Phonation

Once the air has left the lungs, it needs to pass through the larynx [ˈlærɪŋks]. The larynx sits on top of the trachea [trəˈkiːə ‖ ˈtreɪ̯kiə] and is the entrance from the pharynx into the lungs. The primary function of the larynx is protection. The epiglottis is a part of the larynx that looks like a spoon. When a person swallows, a reflex pulls the epiglottis over the larynx, sealing it off from the pharynx, so that no food can accidentally enter the lungs. A man's larynx is visible as the "Adam's apple" at the front of the throat. In order to get an idea of its size, it can be gently pushed left and right with two fingers.

The larynx is a cartilage structure, inside of which the vocal folds are situated. Viewed from above, the vocal folds resemble two sides of a triangle when in resting position. On one side (towards the front of the throat), the vocal folds meet and are fixed. On the other side (towards the rear of the throat), the vocal folds are apart, but attached to the arytenoid cartilages [ˈærɪˌtiːnɔɪd ˈkɑːtəlɪdʒɪz ‖ əˌrɪtənɔɪd ˈkɑːrtəlɪdʒɪz], shown dotted in figures 1 and 2. The arytenoid cartilages can turn on their vertical axis and thus bring the ends of the vocal folds together. If this is the case, the two vocal folds lie next to each other and seal off the passage into the lungs. This again is a matter of protection that is triggered by reflex when a person swallows.

When we speak, it is the two vocal folds that produce voice. The arytenoid cartilages turn and approach the two vocal folds. The space between the vocal folds, the glottis [ˈglɒtɪs ‖ ˈglɑːtəs], is shut. However, air is still

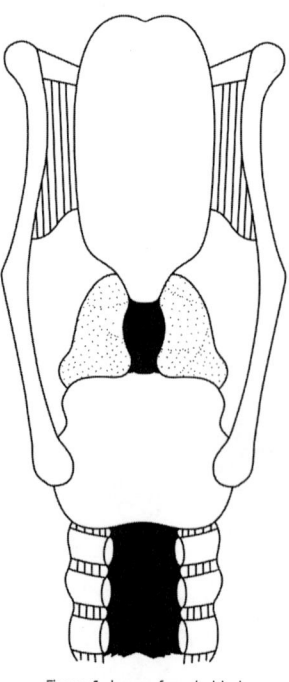

Figure 1: larynx from behind

exhaled from the lungs, so that the pressure rises below the vocal folds. When the pressure becomes too high, the vocal folds are pushed apart. With the glottis now open, the air can escape and the pressure falls. Because of this sudden loss of pressure and because of their own elasticity, the vocal folds are pulled shut again. As the glottis is now closed again, the process repeats from the beginning. This process of phonation is not visible to the naked eye. For low male voices, the glottis opens and

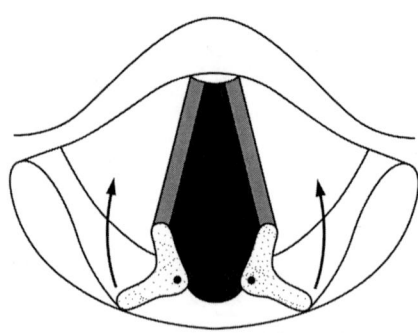

Figure 2: vocal folds and arytenoid cartilages

shuts about 100 times per second, children's voices going into a high register can reach 1200 cycles per second.

Phonation, the production of the primary voice sound, can be felt by comparing a voiceless sound, such as [s] in ⟨sit⟩, to a voiced sound, such as [z] in ⟨zero⟩. Holding the hand to the front of the throat, where the Adam's apple protrudes, a vibration can be felt when saying a long [z]. In the case of [s], no such vibration occurs. Another possibility is to put the cupped hands over both ears. The vibration of the vocal folds can then be heard quite loudly in the case of [z].

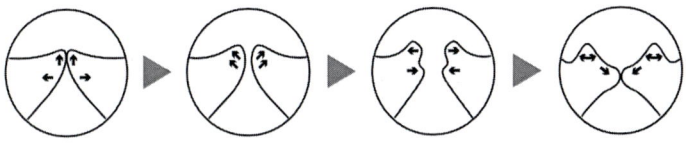

Figure 3: phonation process

While the phase of initiation only provides the source material for speech production with no sound yet, after phonation a primary sound exists. This sound has a certain loudness and also the pitch (how high or low a sound is) is determined here. Also whether the sound is voiced or voiceless is decided now. However, which speech sound or "phone" this sound will finally become, whether it will be an [i], [u], [d] or [m], will only be decided in the following stage: articulation.

Articulation

Articulation is the shaping of air, either with or without voice tone, into speech sounds, so-called phones. When the air has left the larynx, it passes through the pharynx and the mouth or nose, before the speech process is complete.

At the back of the mouth, the velum ['viːləm] is situated. The velum hangs down from the roof of the mouth, allowing air to pass through the nose. This is the case while breathing normally. For speech production, however, the velum can be raised until it touches the back of the throat. In this position, the passage through the nose is sealed off and the air must pass through the mouth instead.

The most important organ in the articulation of speech sounds is the tongue. For both vowels and consonants alike, it is mostly the position and shape of the tongue that determines the sound. The tongue can be divided into different regions: the tip of the tongue is the pointy end that lies behind the lower teeth in the resting position. While the tip is only the very small area at the end of the tongue, the blade refers to the area behind it that stretches over the whole tongue from left to right. The front is the region until roughly the middle of the tongue, while the back is the region starting there. Finally, the root is the area of the tongue that is hidden far back inside the pharynx and anchors the tongue in the jaw.

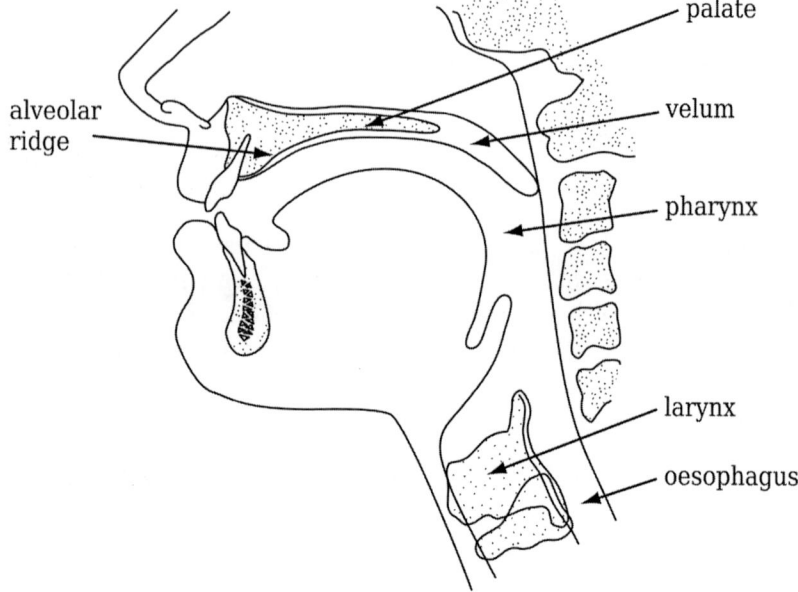

Figure 4: cross-section of the head

The tongue is one of the active articulators, as parts of it move around during the articulation of speech sounds. The passive articulators, on the other hand, are the regions above the tongue. The passive articulators can best be felt by starting with the tip of the tongue behind the upper teeth. The sockets of the teeth, where the teeth finish and the flesh starts, are called alveoles. When pulling the tongue further back, a bump can be felt: the alveolar ridge [ælvi,əʊlə ˈrɪʤ ‖ æl,viːələ˞ ˈrɪʤ]. This is a frequent place of articulation for consonants. Pulling the tongue further backwards, the roof of the mouth can be felt. This area is called the hard palate. (Hard, because there is bone underneath.) Further back starts the velum (or soft palate). The velum can be seen when looking into a mirror with the mouth open. The velum ends with the uvula that hangs like a stalactite from the velum.

In the process of articulation, one of the lower or active articulators (lower lip or one part of the tongue) approaches the upper or passive articulators (area from upper lip to uvula). At which place articulation occurs and to what degree the articulators approach, determines which sound will become audible in the end. For instance, the lower and upper articulators are further apart in the articulation of vowels than they are for consonants.

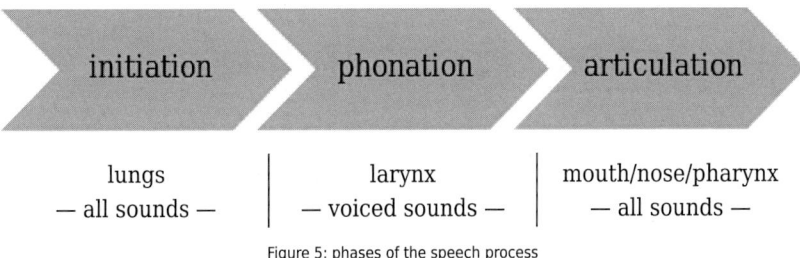

initiation	phonation	articulation
lungs	larynx	mouth/nose/pharynx
— all sounds —	— voiced sounds —	— all sounds —

Figure 5: phases of the speech process

Voiced and Voiceless Sounds

In the stage of phonation, the vocal folds are caused to vibrate by the egressive airstream flowing through them. However, this is not the case for all speech sounds.

Speech sounds can be subdivided into voiced and voiceless sounds. For voiced consonants and all vowels, the vocal folds within the larynx are closed and set into vibration by the airstream flowing through them. For voiceless consonants, the vocal folds are open forming a triangle through which the air can flow unhindered.

A further distinction that goes hand-in-hand with voicing is the distinction between fortis (or tense) and lenis (or lax) sounds. The difference becomes apparent when comparing the sounds [p] and [b]. For fortis consonants, there is high muscular tension in the production of the sound. In the case of [p], the lips are pressed onto one another with considerable force, with the muscles within the lips contracting. Lenis consonants, on the other hand, show a much lower muscular tension. In the case of [b], also both lips are pressed onto one

21

another, but the muscles within the lips are much less contracted. The fortis/ lenis distinction refers to the degree of muscular force in the articulation of consonants. In their canonical realisation, fortis consonants are always voiceless and lenis consonants are always voiced.

Several consonants occur in pairs, where a lenis voiced sound has a fortis voiceless counterpart, for instance [t] and [d]. Other sounds only exist lenis voiced, such as [m]. [h] can only be fortis voiceless.

voiced sounds	voiceless sounds	
[b d g v ð z ʒ ʤ]	[p t k f θ s ʃ ʧ]	with corresponding sound
[m n ŋ l r w j]	—	without corresponding sound
—	[h]	

Table 5: voiced and voiceless sounds

Terminal Devoicing

A few languages including German, Dutch and Russian show complete terminal devoicing. In such languages, whenever a lenis consonant occurs at the end of a syllable, it is pronounced fortis. So although the German conjunction ⟨und⟩ is spelled with ⟨d⟩, it is regularly pronounced [ʔʊnt].

In English, on the other hand, lenis consonants never become fortis. When the spelling indicates a lenis consonant, it is always pronounced lenis voiced, also at the end of a syllable. The conjunction ⟨and⟩ does not just end in writing, but also in spoken language with a [d], not a [t].

German		English	
und	[ʔʊnt]	*and*	[ænd]
Sand	[zant]	*sand*	[sænd]
Trend	[tʁɛnt]	*trend*	[trɛnd]
Club	[klʊp]	*club*	[klʌb]
Bob	[bɔp]	*Bob*	[bɒb]
brav	[bʁaːf]	*brave*	[breɪ̯v]
Fans	[fɛns]	*fans*	[fænz]

Table 6: terminal devoicing in German

While students should always pronounce and transcribe lenis voiced sounds as such, inflections constitute an exception.

Inflections

English knows only very few suffixes which carry grammatical meaning. These are among others (-s) which can stand either for plural, possessive or on verbs for third person singular and (-ed) which can either form the past tense or a participle. These so-called inflectional suffixes need special consideration, as their pronunciation depends on the preceding sound.

In words where the last sound before the suffix is a fortis sound, also the suffix is pronounced fortis: (s) is spoken as [s] and (ed) as [t]. If, on the other hand, the preceding sound is lenis voiced, also the suffix is pronounced lenis: (s) as [z] and (ed) as [d]. In cases where the sound before the suffix is similar to the suffix, rendering the word unpronounceable, an [ɪ] is inserted. So after [s], [z], [ʃ], [ʒ], [tʃ] or [dʒ] the suffix (s) is pronounced [ɪz], after [t] or [d] past or participle (ed) is pronounced as [ɪd].

	(-ed)		**(-s)**	
after voiceless sound	[t]	*liked* [laɪkt]	[s]	*cats* [kæts]
after voiced sound	[d]	*moved* [muːvd]	[z]	*dogs* [dɒgz]
after similar sound	[ɪd]	*sounded* ['saʊndɪd]	[ɪz]	*kisses* ['kɪsɪz]

Table 7: pronunciation of inflectional suffixes

Exercises

2.1

Decide for the sounds in bold print whether they are voiced or voiceless and find the correct IPA symbol.

judge	[ ]	house	[ ]	television	[ ]
his	[ ]	through	[ ]	resolve	[ ]
live	[ ]	because	[ ]	future	[ ]
sister	[ ]	method	[ ]	choose	[ ]
further	[ ]	sure	[ ]	large	[ ]

2.2

The words ⟨their⟩ and ⟨there⟩ are spelt differently, but they have the same pronunciation [ðɛə ‖ ðɛr]. They are homophones. Can you think of other homophones in English?

2.3

If your native language is not English, pronounce the following words and make sure they do not sound alike.

heart – hard	cart – card
hurt – heard	plate – played
kit – kid	fright – fried
life – live	surf – serve
leaf – leave	proof – proove

2.4

Transcribe the following passage from *The Time Machine* by H. G. Wells.

I am afraid I cannot convey the peculiar sensations of time travelling. They are excessively unpleasant. There is a feeling exactly like that one has upon a switchback – of a helpless headlong motion! I felt the same horrible anticipation, too, of an imminent smash. As I put on pace, night followed day like the flapping of a black wing. The dim suggestion of the laboratory seemed presently to fall away from me, and I saw the sun hopping swiftly across the sky, leaping it every minute, and every minute marking a day. I supposed the laboratory had been destroyed and I had come into the open air.

 Listen to a recording of the transcription text online at:
www.phonetiker.net/transcript/

3 Consonants
['kɒnsənənts]

Consonants are sounds that are characterised by an obstruction in the oral cavity. This obstruction is realised by the lower (or active) articulators moving upwards towards the upper (or passive) articulators. The air flowing outwards from the lungs needs to flow over or around this obstacle in the mouth or it may even come to a halt behind it. This leads to turbulences in the airflow, which become audible as noises.

Consonants are either fortis/voiceless or lenis/voiced. Voiceless and voiced says whether the vocal folds vibrate or not. Fortis and lenis, on the other hand, states the articulatory force with which the sounds are produced, whether the muscles involved are tense or lax. In the consonant table, fortis sounds stand on the left hand side, while lenis sounds stand on the right. In addition to tension and voice, the question of where in the mouth (place of articulation) and by what mechanism (manner of articulation) a sound is produced are important for the classification of consonants.

Plosives

Plosives or stops are produced with a complete obstruction of the airflow. For [p] or [b] as an example, both lips are pressed onto one another (bilabial), sealing off the passage through the mouth. At the same time, the velum at the back of the mouth is raised, so that the air cannot escape through the nose either. While air is still flowing outwards from the lungs, the pressure behind the barrier (the lips in the example) rises. When the barrier is finally abandoned, a noise becomes audible that resembles a small explosion, hence the name plosives.

Another position for plosives is alveolar. Here the tip of the tongue touches the alveolar ridge. So in this case, it is not behind the lips, but behind the tongue with the tip resting right above the teeth that the airstream is shut off and cannot flow any further. The sound that becomes audible when this obstacle is released is either [t] or [d].

A last position common in most languages is velar. Here the airstream is cut off even earlier. For velar plosives, the back of the tongue rises until it touches the velum. The sounds from this place of articulation are [k] and [g].

27

	bi-labial	labio-dental	dental	alveolar	post-alveolar	palatal	velar	glottal
English	p b			t d			k g	
other languages						c ɟ		ʔ

Table 8: plosives

The articulation of plosives can be subdivided into three phases. The first phase is obstruction when the articulators move into place. The second phase is occlusion when the air pressure behind the obstacle rises. The last phase is release when the active articulators move away from the passive ones. While in the release phase the explosion noise becomes audible, the first two phases are silent.

In other languages, palatal plosives can also be heard, e.g. in Czech, where orthographically they are represented by ⟨t'⟩ and ⟨d'⟩. Here it is neither the tip nor the back of the tongue that is lifted, but the part in-between, the front sealing off the airstream in the region of the hard palate.

In the articulation of the glottal stop [ʔ], the obstruction is not within the mouth, but inside the larynx. The vocal folds close and stop the airstream before it is again released. The glottal stop can be heard in Estuary English, a relatively young accent associated with the greater London area, where often syllable-final [t] is not pronounced, but replaced by a glottal stop. The word ⟨but⟩ is pronounced like [bʌʔ]. In German, a syllable starting with a vowel is always preceded by a glottal stop. This is a common pronunciation error made by speakers of German as a foreign language who are ignorant of the glottal stop rule. In the case of the word ⟨bearbeiten⟩, the ⟨be-⟩ seems to flow into ⟨-arbeiten⟩ while native speakers of German separate the two vowels by a glottal stop: [bə'ʔaʁbaɛ̯tn̩].

In many American accents, ⟨t⟩ is not pronounced as a plosive when it occurs between two vowels, but as a tap.

Unlike many other languages, in English as well as in German fortis plosives are strongly aspirated in syllable-initial position. Details are given in a later chapter.

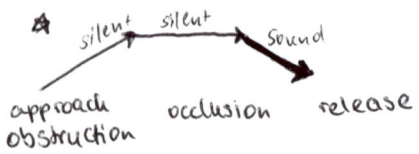

Nasals   → only consonant sounds where the nose is involved

In the case of nasals, the pulmonic airstream does not flow through the mouth, but through the nose. Nasals are sometimes called nasal stops, since they have the same oral closure as plosives. Unlike plosives, nasals only exist as lenis/voiced.

In English, there are three places of articulation for nasals that are the same as for plosives: bilabial, alveolar and velar. Inside the mouth, the articulators move into the same position as for a plosive. However, now the velum at the back of the mouth is lowered and hangs downwards, so that the air flows through the nose rather than through the mouth. With both lips closed, [m] is produced. The tongue tip touching the alveolar ridge leads to [n] and the back of the tongue lifted towards the velum is heard as [ŋ]. [ŋ] is the last sound in the word (thing), in writing usually symbolised by (ng). [ŋ] only occurs in word-final position. The name of this sound is "eng" [ɛŋ].

end of/ after a morpheme   *within morpheme*

	bi-labial	labio-dental	dental	alveolar	post-alveolar	palatal	velar	glottal
English	m			n			ŋ	
other languages		ɱ				ɲ		

Table 9: nasals

In other languages, e.g. French, palatal nasals also exist with the front of the tongue touching the hard palate. It is the sound symbolised by (gn) in the words (cognac) or (vignette).

For labiodental nasals, it is not both lips touching, but rather the lower lip touching the upper teeth. It can be heard in the English word (comfort) or the German word (Senf), where in casual pronunciation the (n) or (m) sounds somehow like [m] or [n] respectively. In fact, it is neither [m] nor [n], but the labiodental nasal [ɱ].

Fricatives

Fricatives are another major sound class that has various places of articulation. Also for fricatives, the lower articulators are raised and approach the upper articulators. Unlike for plosives or nasals, however, the passage through the oral cavity is not sealed off completely. The lower articulators are not fully in contact with the upper articulators, but leave a small gap somewhere. When the airstream is forced through this narrow gap, turbulences occur in the airflow once it has passed this obstacle and these become audible as a friction noise. Fricatives exist both as fortis and lenis consonants.

The concept of friction can best be felt for [f], where the lower lip approaches the upper teeth. Here a coldness on lips and teeth gives an idea of the airflow. The lenis counterpart to fortis [f] is [v], the first sound in ⟨very⟩ or in German ⟨wer⟩.

The typical English ⟨th⟩ is in fact not one sound, but two dental fricatives. For both, the tip of the tongue lies right behind the upper teeth, sometimes even between the teeth. For the fortis dental fricative, as in ⟨thing⟩, the IPA symbol used is [θ] ("theta" ['θiːtə]), while the symbol for the lenis fricative as in ⟨this⟩ is [ð] ("eth" [εð]).

When the tip of the tongue approaches the alveolar ridge, as for [t d n], but only the sides of the tongue make contact with the inner sides of the upper teeth, leaving a narrow gap in the middle of the tongue, the sounds [s] as in ⟨set⟩ or [z] as in ⟨zero⟩ become audible.

Two further fricatives do not correspond to single letters in the English alphabet. [ʃ] ("esh" [εʃ]) is the sound usually symbolised by ⟨sh⟩, as in ⟨shoe⟩. [ʒ] ("zhee" [ʒiː]) is the lenis variant and much rarer in English. It can be found in the middle of the word ⟨vision⟩. For the articulation of these two sounds, a larger area of the tongue, tip and blade, is in near-contact with the roof of the mouth further back than the alveolar ridge and the groove in middle of the tongue is wider.

The last fricative in English is [h]. The place of articulation of [h] is hard to determine. The IPA chart lists it as glottal, but the constriction is rather somewhere in pharynx or larynx.

	bi-labial	labio-dental	dental	alveolar	post-alveolar	palatal	velar	glottal
English		f v	θ ð	s z	ʃ ʒ			h
other languages	ɸ β					ç ʝ	x ɣ	

Table 10: fricatives

In other languages, fricatives exist with a place of articulation further towards the back of the mouth. The German sound heard in ⟨nicht⟩ is the palatal fricative [ç], which exists in English at the start of the word ⟨human⟩. Its lenis counterpart [ʝ] is found in Swedish. Fricatives with a narrow gap between the back of the tongue and the velum are [x] and [ɣ]. The fortis fricative [x] is found in German ⟨Nacht⟩ or in Scottish ⟨loch⟩. The lenis variant of the velar fricative [ɣ] is the standard German pronunciation of the letter ⟨r⟩, although in transcription the symbol [ʁ] is mostly used.

Affricates

Affricates can best be described as a plosive combined with a fricative, both at the same place of articulation (homorganic). The articulation of an affricate begins like a plosive with an obstruction and occlusion phrase. The release phase, however, is slower, so that in this phase a friction noise occurs.

It is debatable whether affricates should be considered as a class of their own or whether they should simply be seen as two sounds in sequence and hence be classified as plosives and fricatives. For a variety of reasons, such as syllabification, it makes sense, however, to assume that English has two affricate sounds: [tʃ] as in ⟨church⟩ and [dʒ] as in ⟨judge⟩.

	bi-labial	labio-dental	dental	alveolar	post-alveolar	palatal	velar	glottal
English					tʃ dʒ			
other languages		pf		ts dz			kx	

Table 11: affricates

In other languages, different combinations of plosives and fricatives can be considered affricates. In German, for instance, the sound sequences [pf] and

[ts] are often classified as affricates, since they behave like one sound rather than two. Italian has also [dz]. In Japanese, the palatalised post-alveolar affricates [tɕ] and [dʑ] can be found.

Approximants

The articulation of approximants is similar to that of fricatives: the lower articulators also approach the upper ones. However, the gap between the two is much wider than for fricatives. As the air can pass through the mouth more or less unhindered, no friction occurs and, hence, no friction noise either. Approximants are always lenis/voiced.

almost as open as vowels

The English ⟨r⟩ belongs to the class of approximants. The tip or blade of the tongue approaches the place behind the alveolar ridge (post-alveolar), but not as far back as the hard palate. The correct IPA symbol for this articulation is [ɹ]. For reasons of simplicity, most books use [r] as the transcription symbol for this sound.

The other two approximants, which are sometimes also called semi-vowels, are [j] as in ⟨yes⟩ and [w] as in ⟨why⟩. For [j] as the only palatal sound of English, the front of the tongue approaches the hard palate. [w] is special in that it has two places of articulation: it is velar, because the back of the tongue is raised towards the velum, but additionally the lips are rounded, making it also labial.

	bi-labial	labio-dental	dental	alveolar	post-alveolar	palatal	labial velar	glottal
English					ɹ	j	w	
other languages		ʋ						

Table 12: approximants

In other languages, also labiodental approximants exist with the lower lip approaching the upper teeth. In Dutch, the words ⟨wee⟩ or ⟨water⟩ are pronounced with a labiodental approximant rather than a fricative.

Laterals

Lateral consonants are usually lateral approximants. For the articulation of laterals, the tongue is in contact with the roof of the mouth. In English, the tip of the tongue rests firmly at the alveolar ridge. However, additionally the sides of tongue are lowered, so that the airstream flows around the left and right side of the tongue rather than over it.

English knows two alveolar lateral approximants: clear and dark /l/. Clear /l/ occurs before vowels in Received Pronunciation. It is the /l/ sound found in most European languages. In all other positions as well as in American accents, a dark /l/ is produced: [ɫ] ("l tilde" [ɛl 'tɪldə]). The [ɫ] sound is velarised, meaning that in addition to the alveolar articulation, the back of the tongue is raised towards the velum. In transcription, the difference between clear and dark /l/ is usually not transcribed, as it can can be inferred from the position of the sound within a word.

	bi-labial	labio-dental	dental	alveolar	post-alveolar	palatal	velar	glottal
English				l				
other languages						ʎ	ʟ	

Table 13: laterals

In other languages, lateral approximants with other places of articulation can be found. In Spanish, the digraph ⟨ll⟩ stands for the palatal lateral approximant [ʎ], as for instance in ⟨million⟩.

Lateral fricatives (not in the table) are also articulated with a lowering of the sides of the tongue. But the gap between active and passive articulators is smaller than for lateral approximants, leading to a friction noise. Welsh knows the voiceless alveolar lateral fricative [ɬ] ("belted l"). It can be found in many place names, that often start with ⟨Llan⟩, meaning "church". To a German ear, it sounds like an [l] and the sound in German ⟨nicht⟩ articulated at the same time.

 Listen to a recording of the longest place name with [ɬ] online at: llanfairpwllgwyngyllgogerychwyrndrobwllllantysiliogogogoch.co.uk

Taps and Trills

The articulation of taps is similar to plosives in that the lower articulators come into direct contact with the upper ones. However, while plosives have an occlusion phase during which the air pressure is allowed to rise behind the obstacle, this phase is missing in the articulation of taps: the lower articulators move away right after having come into contact.

In English, we find an alveolar tap, the tip of the tongue briefly touching the alveolar ridge. In Scottish English, the ⟨r⟩ is pronounced as an alveolar tap. It is also the ⟨r⟩ realisation heard in many Southern German regions.

	bi-labial	labio-dental	dental	alveolar	post-alveolar	palatal	velar	glottal
English				ɾ				
other languages		ѵ						

Table 14: taps

In many American accents, ⟨t⟩ is realised as an alveolar tap in words such as ⟨writing⟩, making it sound somewhat like ⟨riding⟩, though not quite. This phenomenon is called [t]-voicing and can be transcribed as [ɾ].

For a trill, lower and upper articulators come into brief contact, however, not just once as for taps, but several times in rapid succession. Spanish has an alveolar trill in the word ⟨perro⟩ in opposition to the word ⟨pero⟩, which is pronounced with an alveolar tap.

	bi-labial	labio-dental	dental	alveolar	post-alveolar	palatal	velar	glottal
plosives	p b			t d			k g	ʔ
nasals	m			n			ŋ	
fricatives		f v	θ ð	s z	ʃ ʒ			h
affricates					ʧ ʤ			
approxi-mants				ɹ		j	labial / w	
laterals				l				
taps				ɾ				

Table 15: English consonants

Further Places of Articulation

As can be seen in the full IPA chart below, there are further places of articulation that have not been discussed so far, as they do not play a role in English phonology.

CONSONANTS (PULMONIC)   © 2005 IPA

	Bilabial	Labiodental	Dental	Alveolar	Postalveolar	Retroflex	Palatal	Velar	Uvular	Pharyngeal	Glottal
Plosive	p b			t d		ʈ ɖ	c ɟ	k g	q ɢ		ʔ
Nasal	m	ɱ		n		ɳ	ɲ	ŋ	ɴ		
Trill	ʙ			r					ʀ		
Tap or Flap		ⱱ		ɾ		ɽ					
Fricative	ɸ β	f v	θ ð	s z	ʃ ʒ	ʂ ʐ	ç ʝ	x ɣ	χ ʁ	ħ ʕ	h ɦ
Lateral fricative				ɬ ɮ							
Approximant		ʋ		ɹ		ɻ	j	ɰ			
Lateral approximant				l		ɭ	ʎ	ʟ			

Where symbols appear in pairs, the one to the right represents a voiced consonant. Shaded areas denote articulations judged impossible.

Table 16: full IPA consonant table

Plosives, nasals, trills and fricatives can be articulated further back than the velum, at the uvula. Uvular plosives, for instance, can be found in Standard Arabic.

For pharyngeal fricatives, the constriction is even further back: the constriction is between the root of the tongue and the back wall of the pharynx.

Retroflex sounds are articulated with the tongue curled around, so that the underside of the tip points upwards in the region of the hard palate. Scandinavian languages, such as Swedish and Norwegian, have retroflex plosives [ʈ] and [ɖ], e.g. Swedish (karta). In several American regions, ⟨r⟩ is articulated as a retroflex sound [ɻ].

Listen to recordings of the pulmonic consonants online at: www.phonetiker.net/transcript/

Additional Terminology

In other books on phonetics, additional or alternative terminology may be used that shall only be briefly mentioned here:
- stops: plosives (sometimes also affricates and/or nasals)
- obstruents: plosives, affricates and fricatives
- sonorants: nasals and approximants including [l]
- semi-vowels or glides: [j] and [w]
- liquids: [l] and [r]
- frictionless continuant: [r]
- flaps: similar to taps

Letter to Sound

⟨s⟩ as [s] and [z]

⟨s⟩ can be pronounced either fortis voiceless [s] or lenis voiced [z]. Students sometimes find it hard to tell the two sounds apart. One reason is that the two sounds have a different distribution in English than in German, meaning they are found at different positions within a word.

The most problematic position for English learners with a German background is ⟨s⟩ at the beginning of a word. In English, word-initial ⟨s⟩ is always pronounced fortis voiceless, as in ⟨sand⟩ [sænd]. (Only words that have ⟨z⟩ in the spelling are pronounced lenis voiced, as in ⟨zero⟩ [ˈzɪɐ̯rəʊ̯ ‖ ˈzɪroʊ̯].) In German, on the other hand, it is exactly the other way round: word-initial ⟨s⟩ is always pronounced lenis voiced, as in ⟨Sand⟩ [zant].

In the middle of a word, the pronunciation of ⟨s⟩ is usually [z], in words such as ⟨busy⟩ or ⟨easy⟩. It is [s] in words of foreign origin, as for instance ⟨crisis⟩ or ⟨inclusive⟩.

Word-final ⟨s⟩ is most usually pronounced [s], for example in words like ⟨bus⟩ or ⟨else⟩. Function words, such as ⟨is⟩, ⟨has⟩ or ⟨as⟩, are an exception and are pronounced with a lenis voiced [z]. Also verbs ending in ⟨-se⟩, such as ⟨close⟩, have lenis voiced pronunciation. Plural, genitive and third-person ⟨s⟩ are voiced if the preceding sound is voiced.

⟨th⟩

The letter combination ⟨th⟩ must always be pronounced as a dental fricative, never as [d] or [s]. There are very few exceptions where ⟨th⟩ is pronounced [t], e.g. the river Thames or the name Thomas are pronounced [tɛmz] and ['tɒməs ‖ 'tɑːməs] respectively.

As to the question of whether ⟨th⟩ is pronounced fortis voiceless [θ] or lenis voiced [ð], the general rules are more or less the same as for ⟨s⟩: at the beginning or end of a word, usually the fortis voiceless fricative will occur, within a word it is more likely that the lenis voiced one can be found. Exceptions are function words, such as ⟨this, that, there⟩ which start with a lenis voiced fricative. Foreign words of Greek origin, as for instance ⟨hypothesis⟩ or ⟨anthem⟩, generally have the fortis voiceless fricative.

⟨ng⟩

The letter combination ⟨ng⟩ is pronounced as the velar nasal [ŋ]. However, depending on the internal structure of a word, a [g] is also pronounced in some words, in others it is not. The decisive question is whether ⟨ng⟩ occurs at the end of a meaningful unit or not.

The word ⟨singer⟩, for example, can be decomposed into the verb {sing} and the suffix {er}, which transforms the verb into an agent noun. In this case, ⟨ng⟩ stands at the end of the meaningful unit {sing} and therefore [g] is not pronounced. The pronunciation of ⟨singer⟩ is ['sɪŋə ‖ 'sɪŋɚ].

Other words, such as ⟨finger⟩ or ⟨English⟩, cannot be split up into smaller units. This means that ⟨ng⟩ is not at the end of a meaningful unit, but right inside it. In such cases, a [g] is inserted after the nasal. The pronunciation of ⟨finger⟩ is ['fɪŋgə ‖ 'fɪŋgɚ], ⟨English⟩ is pronounced ['ɪŋglɪʃ].

Also for the comparative or superlative forms of adjectives, a [g] enters the pronunciation. So the adjective ⟨young⟩, ⟨younger⟩ and ⟨youngest⟩ is pronounced [jʌŋ], ['jʌŋgə ‖ 'jʌŋgɚ] and ['jʌŋgɪst] respectively.

⟨w⟩ and ⟨v⟩

The IPA symbols [w] and [v] correspond exactly to the letters ⟨w⟩ and ⟨v⟩. Wherever ⟨v⟩ is written, it is pronounced as the labiodental fricative that is also found in German ⟨wenn⟩. Wherever ⟨w⟩ occurs in the spelling, the pronunciation is the typically English [w] sound with rounded lips.

⟨r⟩

The letter ⟨r⟩ is not always pronounced in all accents. In many so-called non-rhotic accents, such as Received Pronunciation, ⟨r⟩ is not pronounced when it occurs after a vowel. In rhotic accents, on the other hand, such as General American, ⟨r⟩ is always pronounced whenever it occurs in the spelling.

In non-rhotic accents, there are different possibilities for the realisation of ⟨r⟩. In some words, centring diphthongs occur instead. For instance, the words ⟨here⟩ and ⟨there⟩ are pronounced [hɪə̯] and [ðɛə̯]. In other words, the ⟨r⟩ is not pronounced at all, so that ⟨car⟩ and ⟨more⟩ become [kɑː] and [mɔː].

In rhotic accents, the mid central vowels [ə] and [ɜː] deserve special attention when ⟨r⟩ occurs in the spelling. Here the ⟨r⟩ is pronounced, however not after the vowel, but the articulation movement occurs simultaneously with the vowel, so that it receives an 'r-colouring', which is transcribed as [ɚ] and [ɝː].

⟨c⟩ and ⟨g⟩

As a general rule, the pronunciation of the letters ⟨c⟩ and ⟨g⟩ depends on the following vowel. If the following vowel letter is ⟨a, o, u⟩, the articulation is velar: ⟨c⟩ is pronounced as [k] and ⟨g⟩ as [g], for instance in ⟨cat⟩ and ⟨go⟩. If on the other hand the following vowel is ⟨e, i, y⟩, the pronunciation is [s] for ⟨c⟩ and [dʒ] for ⟨g⟩, such as in ⟨city⟩ and ⟨magic⟩. Especially for ⟨g⟩, however, there are many exception, as for instance ⟨get⟩ or ⟨give⟩.

Exercises

3.1

Transcribe the consonant sounds you hear in the following words. All words contain silent consonants, so that not every letter corresponds to an IPA symbol.

chalk	thumb	receipt	knock	dough	salmon	Wednesday
debt	calm	honest	wrap	subtle	yacht	mnemonics
vehicle	gnome	damn	calve	muscle	ghost	handsome
womb	weigh	psycho	isle	solemn	wrist	sovereign
doubt	sign	reign	tomb	hour	folk	heir

3.2

Which is the correct IPA symbol for the letters in bold print?

enough	[g]	[gh]	[f]	[w]
action	[tʃ]	[ʒ]	[ts]	[ʃ]
chips	[c]	[tʃ]	[ʃ]	[dʒ]
occasion	[z]	[ʃ]	[s]	[ʒ]
accent	[ks]	[cs]	[s]	[ʃ]
scheme	[ʃ]	[h]	[k]	[tʃ]

3.3

The first words children produce usually sound like (mama) or (papa). Based on your knowledge of the articulation of consonants, can you imagine why?

3.4

Transcribe the following passage from *Gulliver's Travels* by Jonathan Swift.

I attempted to rise, but was not able to stir: for, as I happened to lie on my back, I found my arms and legs were strongly fastened on each side to the ground. I heard a confused noise about me; but in the posture I lay, could see nothing except the sky. In a little time I felt something alive moving on my left leg, which advancing gently forward over my breast, came almost up to my chin; when, bending my eyes downwards as much as I could, I perceived it to be a human creature not six inches high, with a bow and arrow in his hands, and a quiver at his back.

 Listen to a recording of the transcription text online at: www.phonetiker.net/transcript/

3.5

If you are not a native speaker of English, train your pronunciation of ⟨th⟩ in consonant clusters with ⟨s⟩-sounds.

[sθ]	[sð]	[zθ]	[zð]
nice thing	*pass this*	*wise thought*	*choose this*
pass through	*kiss those*	*whose thing*	*he's though*
mass theory	*miss that*	*his threat*	*sneeze there*

[θs]	[θz]	[ðs]	[ðz]
bath sink	*death zone*	*breathe slowly*	*smooth xerox*
math session	*depth zoom*	*clothe someone*	*loathe zebras*
fourth seat	*cloth zipper*	*soothe sunburn*	*smooth zoom*

4 Vowels
['vaʊəlz]

Vowels are speech sounds of opening: there is no obstruction in the oral cavity. The tongue approaches the upper articulators to a far lesser degree than for consonants, so that there is no obstruction. The airstream, which has passed through the closed vocal folds and caused them to vibrate, can pass through the mouth more or less unhindered. Therefore, vowels contain no friction or explosion noise that is typical for many consonants. Vowels are always voiced.

The different vowel sounds of all languages differ in three main criteria: height of tongue, part of tongue and lip-rounding.

Lip-rounding is the most easily discernible criterion, because it can be seen by looking into a mirror. When saying [i] as in (see), the lips are spread, almost into a flat line. When saying [u] as in (you), the lips are rounded, as if attempting a kiss.

Height of tongue describes how far the jaw is open or closed and accordingly to which degree the tongue is lowered or raised. When saying [a] like at the doctor, the jaw is maximally open and also the tongue is pulled downwards. In contrast, when saying [i], the mouth is quite closed and additionally the front of the tongue rises towards the palatal region.

Part of tongue as the last main criterion is harder to see or feel. When saying [i] and [u] in rapid alternation, the tongue appears to be sliding back and forth inside the mouth. This is because different regions of the tongue are raised in different directions. When saying [i], the front of the tongue rises forward towards the palatal region. When saying [u], the back of the tongue rises backward towards the velum.

In addition to these three main criteria, different languages use further criteria for the classification of vowels. Tension may play a role, with some vowels articulated with a higher muscular effort than others. In English, also length is decisive with some vowels being long, while others are short.

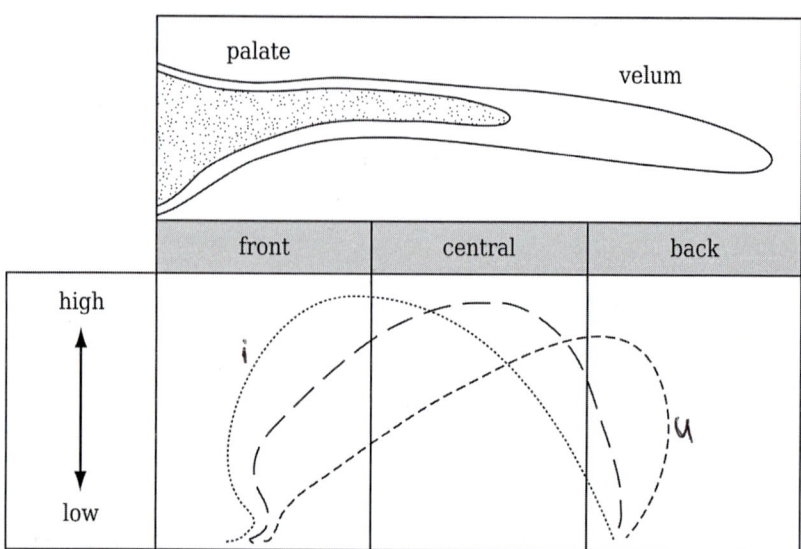

Figure 6: position of tongue for front, central and back vowels

Cardinal Vowels

In order to be able to describe vowels, a reference system was established by the British phonetician Daniel Jones: the system of cardinal vowels. Cardinal vowels are language-independent and clearly defined vowel qualities, against which the vowels of all languages of the world are compared. At the same time, the cardinal vowels define the outside borders of the space within which vowels can be articulated.

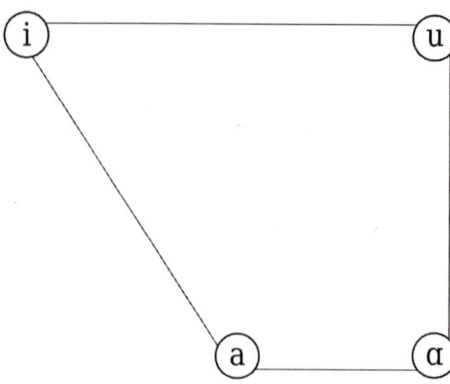

Figure 7: outer corners of the vowel space

Cardinal vowel 1 is [i] as in French (il). This sound is similar to the sound in German (ihm) or English (we), but the tongue is raised still a bit higher. [i] defines the upper front corner of the vowel space. The mouth is as closed as possible for a vowel and the front of the tongue is maximally raised. If the tongue were raised any higher, friction would occur and the resulting sound would need to be classified as a consonant. No vowel can be further front or high than [i].

The highest, but back cardinal vowel is [u]. Here the back of the tongue is raised as high as possible towards the velum. This sound corresponds to the sound in German (Kuh) or French (ou).

The sound in English (father) corresponds to another cardinal vowel: [ɑ] ("script a"). It sounds much darker than the (a)-sounds in many other languages, because the tongue is retracted and lies further back in the mouth. [ɑ] is the lowest possible and most retracted vowel articulation possible.

[a] is the cardinal vowel of the lower front corner. The vowel of German (Mann) or French (femme) is more central. For the cardinal vowel [a] the tongue is further to the front. In the dialects of Northern Germany, [a] approaches the acoustic quality of this cardinal vowel.

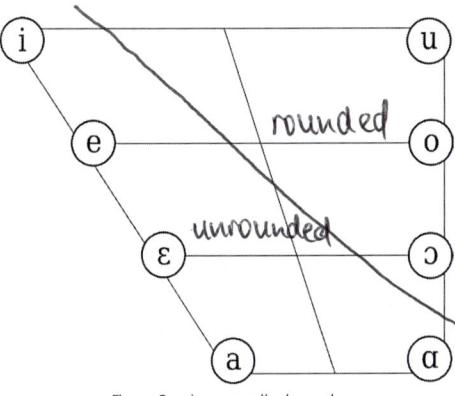

Figure 8: primary cardinal vowels

There are four more cardinal vowels that divide the distance between [i] and [a] at the front and [u] and [ɑ] at the back into thirds.

The cardinal vowel [e] lies one third down from [i]. This cardinal vowel corresponds to the vowels in German (See) or French (été).

One third up from [a] is cardinal vowel [ɛ] ("epsilon"). The words (nett) in German, (bête) in French or (это) in Russian contain this vowel.

At the back [o] has roughly the same height as [e] at the front and is one third down from [u]. It occurs in the German word (so) or in French in the word (eau).

The last cardinal vowel is [ɔ] ("open o"), which has roughly the same height as [ɛ] at the front and is one third up from [ɑ]. This vowel can be heard in German (oft) or in French (homme).

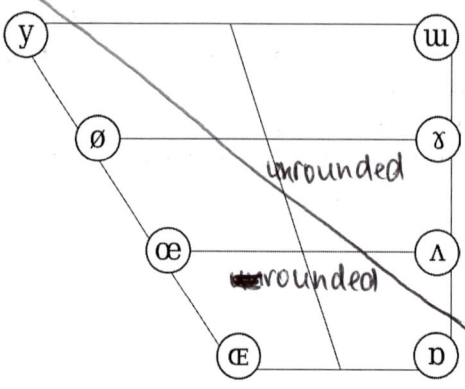

Figure 9: secondary cardinal vowels

These cardinal vowels are more precisely the primary cardinal vowels, because we still have to take lip-rounding into consideration. In case of the primary cardinal vowels, the back vowels except [ɑ] have all lip-rounding, while the front vowels and [ɑ] are unrounded. There is a second set of cardinal vowels, the secondary cardinal vowels. These have exactly the same position as the primary cardinal vowels, but their lip-rounding is reversed: the front vowels are rounded and the back vowels are not.

At the position of [i], but with rounded lips, is [y], which can be found in German (für) or French (tu). The higher mid secondary cardinal vowel is [ø] as in German (schön) or in French (deux). At lower mid position is [œ], the sound in German (können) or in French (neuf). The secondary cardinal vowels of the back are much more seldom in the languages of the world. Turkish (ılık) has [ɯ], for instance, even though more centralised.

English Monophthongs

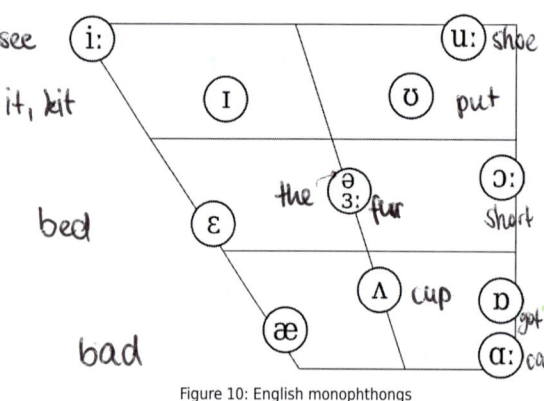

Figure 10: English monophthongs

A monophthong is a steady-state vowel. During its articulation, the speech organs remain at the same position, so that the vowel sounds the same from beginning to end. In addition to the criteria of height of tongue, part of tongue and lip-rounding, length and tension also play a role in English.

In transcription, length is indicated by [ː] after the vowel. All long vowels are also tense, while the short vowels are all lax. The difference between tense and lax vowels can be felt when comparing the vowels in the words ⟨food⟩ and ⟨foot⟩. While for the tense vowel in the word ⟨food⟩ or in German ⟨Fuß⟩, the contraction of the muscles within the lips can be felt, this is far less so in the word ⟨foot⟩ or in German ⟨Fluss⟩ that both contain a lax vowel.

In all, English distinguishes between twelve monophthongs. Compared with the languages of the world, that is quite a high number. Spanish, for instance, manages with just five monophthongs. German, on the other hand, distinguishes between 16 monophthongs.

[iː] and [ɪ]

high   lower high

English has a sound that is a little lower than cardinal vowel [i]. Still the same symbol is used for it. The English vowel [iː] is long and occurs for instance in ⟨we⟩. In English, there is also a short vowel [ɪ] ("small capital i") as in ⟨it⟩, which is also found in German ⟨im⟩. In the articulation of [ɪ] the tongue is a little lower ("lower high") and further to the centre compared to [iː]. Furthermore, [ɪ] is shorter and the muscles are less tense than in the articulation of [iː].

While [iː] is always long and [ɪ] always short, a third variant [i] can be found in weak forms of function words and words that have undergone a phenomenon called "happy"-tensing. Words such as ⟨happy⟩, ⟨beauty⟩ or the numbers above 20 were originally pronounced with a short [ɪ] at the end: ['hæpɪ], ['bjuːtɪ] and ['twentɪ]. This pronunciation can still be found in many English accents and the Queen, for instance, pronounces these words with a short [ɪ]. For the majority of speakers, however, these words have undergone tensing, meaning lax [ɪ] became tense [i]. That is the reason why in these words we find a tense vowel that is short: ['hæpi], ['bjuːti] and ['twenti].

[uː] and [ʊ]

high   lower high

At the back, the long English vowel [uː] is slightly more central than the cardinal vowel. It is the vowel in ⟨you⟩. The short vowel [ʊ] ("reversed omega") is found in ⟨put⟩ or in German ⟨muss⟩. Similar to [ɪ], it is lower and more centralised than [uː] and also shorter and lax.

Similar to short tense [i], although much rarer, [uː] occurs short in some words, as for instance ⟨influence⟩ ['ɪnfluəns].

45

[ɛ] and [ɔ:]

(front) mid   mid *(back)*

There are two vowels in English that are problematic for transcription. It is the short vowel in ⟨get⟩ and the long vowel in ⟨caught⟩. The position of the ⟨get⟩ vowel is in-between cardinal vowel [e] and [ɛ]. The position of the vowel in ⟨caught⟩ is in the middle between cardinal [o] and [ɔ]. At both these positions, there is no IPA symbol. Of course, there are diacritics: [ẹ] means lower than [e] and [ɛ̣] higher than [ɛ]. But it would be highly inconvenient having to write these all the time.

For reasons of simplicity, one of the cardinal vowel symbols is borrowed, even though the positions do not exactly match. The vowel in ⟨get⟩ is hence transcribed as [ɛ], the vowel in caught as [ɔ:]. Many dictionaries also transcribe ⟨get⟩ with the symbol [e].

[æ]

higher low

[æ] ("ash" [æʃ]) is a short higher low vowel at the front. It occurs, for instance, in ⟨bad⟩. It contrasts with [ɛ] in ⟨bed⟩ where the jaw is much more open and the position of the tongue is lower. Native speakers of German find it difficult to distinguish between ⟨bed⟩ and ⟨bad⟩ or ⟨dead⟩ and ⟨Dad⟩, because German has no sounds at these positions. However, the two vowels in English ⟨dead⟩ and ⟨Dad⟩ are roughly as far apart as the German vowels in ⟨denn⟩ and ⟨dann⟩. So claiming that ⟨dead⟩ and ⟨Dad⟩ sound the same, would be like saying that ⟨denn⟩ and ⟨dann⟩ are identical words.

Schwa   nurse

[ə] and [ɜ:]

central

In the middle of the vowel chart, there are two sounds: short [ə] ("schwa" [ʃwɑ:]) and long [ɜ:] ("reversed epsilon"). This is the <u>resting position</u> of the tongue. It is neither raised nor lowered, neither fronted nor retracted. It is the sound of ⟨e⟩ in the English word ⟨the⟩ before consonants or in the German word ⟨bitte⟩.

The central long vowel [ɜ:] occurs in words where in the spelling a vowel is followed by ⟨r⟩, such as ⟨nurse⟩. It has the same vowel quality as [ə], but is longer. [ɜ:] has no lip-rounding and must not be confused with the sounds represented by ⟨ö⟩ in German or ⟨eu⟩ in French that are rounded front vowels.

[ə] <u>never</u> occurs in a stressed syllable

[ə] and [ɜ:] differ in their position within a word. [ə] unlike all other vowels only ever occurs in unstressed syllables. [ɜ:], on the other hand, is mostly found in a syllable that is stressed.

In General American, when an ⟨r⟩ follows [ə] and [ɜ:], the sounds become "R-coloured" or rhoticised. Instead of pronouncing two separate sounds (first [ə]/[ɜ:], then [r]), the tip or blade of the tongue that rises for the articulation of [r], already does so during the articulation of the vowel. The vowel receives an R-colouring that is transcribed with the symbols [ɚ] and [ɝ:].

[ʌ]

The cup sound is the vowel heard in the word ⟨cup⟩, transcribed as [ʌ] ("reversed v"). Like [ə], it is a central vowel with no lip-rounding, but the position of the tongue is higher low. It is not as low as German [a], which is a low vowel.

There are several words in English ("the worry words") that contain the letter ⟨o⟩, but where the pronunciation is that of [ʌ]:
above, accompany, among, borough, brother, colour, come, comfort(able), company, compass, cover, covet, done, dozen, front, glove, govern, honey, London, love, Monday, money, monk, monkey, month, mother, none, nothing, one, onion, other, oven, shove, shovel, slovenly, smother, some, son, sponge, stomach, thorough, ton, tongue, won, wonder, worry (GA [wɝ:ri])

[ɒ]
higher low
In addition to long [ɔ:] as in ⟨court⟩ and the sound heard in ⟨so⟩, which is a diphthong, English has another ⟨o⟩ sound: the short [ɒ] ("reversed script a") as in ⟨stop⟩. [ɒ] is a higher low and rounded back vowel. While this vowel is found in the Received Pronunciation of British English, Americans either pronounce the same words with an unrounded [ɑ:] where the tongue is in a low position or they use the [ɔ:] vowel in these words.

[ɑ:]
low, unrounded
Another English vowel that approximates a cardinal vowel is [ɑ:]. It is the vowel heard in the word ⟨father⟩. The tongue position is back and low. [ɑ:] is pronounced without lip-rounding.

47

	tongue height	part of tongue	lip position	length	jaw opening
[iː]	high	front	unrounded	long	close
[ɪ]	lower high	front-central	unrounded	short	semi-close
[ɛ]	mid	front	unrounded	short	mid
[æ]	higher low	front	unrounded	short	semi-open
[ɜː]	mid	central	unrounded	long	mid
[ə]	mid	central	unrounded	short	mid
[ʌ]	higher low	central	unrounded	short	semi-open
[uː]	high	back	rounded	long	close
[ʊ]	lower high	back-central	rounded	short	semi-close
[ɔː]	mid	back	rounded	long	mid
[ɒ]	higher low	back	rounded	short	semi-open
[ɑː]	low	back	unrounded	long	open

Table 17: parameters of English monophthongs

Vowel length is decisive in English. Long vowels, such as [ɔː], are always long and short vowels, as for instance [ɛ], are always short. The IPA symbol for length [ː] should therefore be learnt together with the vowel symbol.

Short vowels are lax, i.e. compared to long vowels which are tense, they are articulated with less muscular tension. For instance, the lips are far less spread or rounded for [ɪ] and [ʊ] than they are for [iː] and [uː] and generally the muscles are more relaxed. While this is not important for transcription or the sound system of English, it becomes important when teaching English vowels to foreign language learners of languages, such as French or Russian, that do not have short [ɪ] or [ʊ] in their native language.

Short vowels are furthermore checked in English, while long vowels are free. This means that when short vowels occur in a stressed syllable, the syllable cannot end with the vowel, but another consonant must follow. That is why words of one syllable can only end with a long and not a short vowel. Words such as [tiː], [dɔː], [tuː] or [kɑː] exist: ⟨tea⟩, ⟨door⟩, ⟨two⟩ and ⟨car⟩, whereas words like [tɪ], [dɒ] or [kʌ], on the other hand, are not possible, only when another consonant follows as in ⟨tin⟩, ⟨dot⟩ or ⟨cut⟩.

Full Vowel Chart and Terminology

The horizontal position of vowels is specified by the part of tongue as either front, central or back. For the vertical dimension, either the highest elevation of the tongue or the degree of jaw opening can be specified.

high	close
lower high	semi-close
upper mid	close mid
mid	mid
lower mid	open mid
higher low	semi-open
low	open

Figure 11: terminology for vowel height

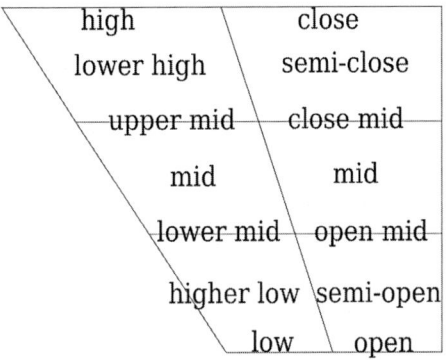

VOWELS

Where symbols appear in pairs, the one
to the right represents a rounded vowel.

Figure 12: full IPA vowel chart, © IPA 2005

Listen to recordings of Cardinal and English vowels online at:
www.phonetiker.net/transcript/

English Diphthongs

Diphthongs are characterised by a gliding movement of the tongue. While for monophthongs, the tongue remains in the same position, for diphthongs, its position changes gradually during the articulation. Since there is a change in place of articulation, the sound that is produced also changes accordingly: diphthongs have a different sound quality at the beginning than at the end.

Diphthongs do not have separate transcription symbols. Rather the starting and end position of the gliding movement are transcribed. To indicate that the two symbols represent a diphthong rather than two monophthongs in a row, a bow can be put under the second vowel. This is the symbol for "non-syllabic", meaning that the second vowel does not create a new syllable, which a monophthong would. The word ⟨neon⟩ ['niːɒn ‖ 'niːɑːn] contains two consecutive monophthongs and thus has two syllables, whereas the word ⟨nine⟩ [na͜ɪn] has only one syllable, because the diphthong must be regarded as one sound, even though the symbol is a digraph.

English distinguishes between closing and centring diphthongs, although centring diphthongs are only found in non-rhotic accents, such as RP. The attributes closing and centring refer to the movement of the tongue: for closing diphthongs, the tongue moves upwards and the mouth closes. For centring diphthongs, on the other hand, the tongue moves towards the centre of the mouth.

Closing diphthongs

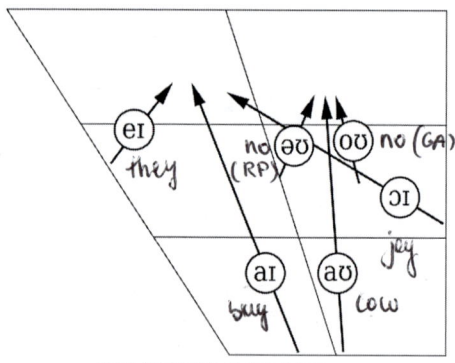

Figure 13: English closing diphthongs

Closing diphthongs show an upward movement of the tongue. In English, closing diphthongs end in either [ɪ] or [ʊ].

The closing diphthongs of English are:

- [aɪ] as in ⟨why⟩
- [eɪ] as in ⟨they⟩
- [ɔɪ] as in ⟨boy⟩
- [aʊ] as in ⟨how⟩ and
- [əʊ] as in ⟨so⟩.

The pronunciation of the latter does not start quite as central in General American: here the pronunciation is [oʊ̯].

Centring diphthongs   *only received pronunciation*

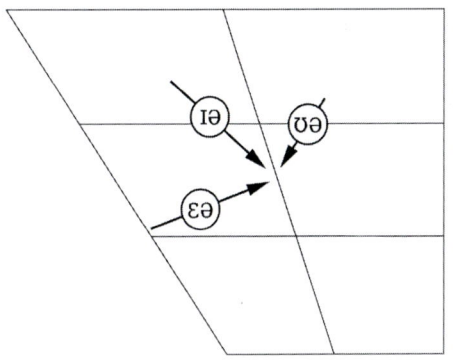

Figure 14: RP centring diphthongs

The gliding movement of centring diphthongs is directed towards the centre of the mouth, towards [ə]. The centring diphthongs are a result of the omission of [r] after vowels. Received Pronunciation knows three centring diphthongs:
- [ɪə̯] as in ⟨here⟩
- [ɛə̯] as in ⟨there⟩ and
- [ʊə̯] as in ⟨cure⟩.

The diphthong [ɛə̯] becomes increasingly pronounced as a long monophthong [ðɛ:].

Rhotic accents, such as General American, pronounce [r] also in postvocalic position. Therefore, such accents have no centring diphthongs. ⟨here⟩, for instance, is pronounced [hɪr].

British vs. American Pronunciation

The US American standard pronunciation, General American, differs slightly in the inventory of vowels from the Received Pronunciation of Britain. While in some cases, it is only a single vowel that sounds different, other differences need more consideration.

The closing diphthong [əʊ̯] does not start in the centre, but more to the back, roughly in the middle between [ə] and [ɔ:] and therefore sounds rather like [oʊ̯].

Another difference arises from the rhotic character of General American: ⟨r⟩ after vowels is not pronounced in RP, but it is in GA. For [ə] and [ɜ:], however, the articulatory movement of [r] occurs not after, but during the articulation of the vowel, so that these vowels become rhoticised: [ɚ] and [ɝ:]. Yet plain schwa [ə] also exists in GA when a vowel is not followed by ⟨r⟩, as in ⟨drama⟩ [ˈdrɑːmə].

The case of [ɑ:] and [æ] is not so clear-cut. It is well known that words like ⟨dance⟩ and ⟨chance⟩ (the BATH words) are pronounced [dɑ:ns] and [tʃɑ:ns] in RP, while GA still has the older forms [dæns] and [tʃæns] that can also be heard in the North of England. But not all words that contain [ɑ:] in RP automatically have [æ] in GA. The word ⟨father⟩ is pronounced with [ɑ:] in both varieties. Similarly, there are words, such as ⟨arrow⟩, that have [æ] in both RP and GA.

The higher low back vowel [ɒ] does not exist in General American. In most words, where this vowel occurs in RP, the American standard has low [ɑ:], but not in all. In words where the vowel is followed by a voiceless fricative [θ f s] or velar [ŋ g], [ɑ:] can occur, but there is a strong preference for [ɔ:] in these words.

	🇬🇧	🇺🇸
TRAP, ham, cab	[æ]	[æ]
BATH, staff, half	[ɑ:]	
PALM, father, drama		[ɑ:]
LOT, stop, honest	[ɒ]	
CLOTH, long, origin		[ɔ:]
THOUGHT, jaw, all	[ɔ:]	
GOAT, road, so	[əʊ̞]	[oʊ̞]
NURSE, shirt, earth	[ɜ:]	[ɝ:]
AGO, sofa, comma	[ə]	[ə]
LETTER, browser		[ɚ]

Table 18: British and American vowel differences, reference word in small capitals

Letter to Sound

The relationship between letters and sounds for vowels is not as straightforward as it is for consonants. It is therefore advisable not to rely on the written form of a word but to follow one's hearing.

In addition to the vowel qualities specified in the table below, vowels in unstressed syllables often become reduced to schwa [ə], as will be illustrated for the weak forms of function words.

		regular pronunciation			followed by (r)			other		
		🇬🇧	🇺🇸		🇬🇧	🇺🇸		🇬🇧	🇺🇸
(a)	*cap*	[kæp]		*car*	[kɑː]	[kɑːr]	*after*	['ɑːftə]	['æftɚ]
	cape	[keɪp]		*care*	[kɛə]	[kɛr]	*watch*	[wɒtʃ]	[wɑːtʃ]
							warm	[wɔːm]	[wɔːrm]
(e)	*bed*	[bɛd]		*serve*	[sɜːv]	[sɝːv]	*pretty*	['prɪti]	
	secret	['siːkrɪt]		*here*	[hɪə]	[hɪr]	*ballet*	['bæleɪ]	
				there	[ðɛə]	[ðɛr]			
(i)	*bit*	[bɪt]		*firm*	[fɜːm]	[fɝːm]	*machine*	[məˈʃiːn]	
	bite	[baɪt]		*fire*	['faɪə]	['faɪɚ]			
(o)	*not*	[nɒt]	[nɑːt]	*door*	[dɔː]	[dɔːr]	*come*	[kʌm]	
	note	[nəʊt]	[noʊt]	*work*	[wɜːk]	[wɝːk]	*cross*	[krɒs]	[krɔːs]
							move	[muːv]	
(u)	*cup*	[kʌp]		*pure*	[pjʊə]	[pjʊr]	*push*	[pʊʃ]	
	music	['mjuːzɪk]		*turn*	[tɜːn]	[tɝːn]			

Table 19: letter-to-sound relations for vowels

Weak Forms

The syllables in a word can be either stressed (or accentuated) or they remain unstressed. In English, vowels in unstressed syllables become reduced in length and obscured in quality, most often to schwa [ə]. The word (actor), for instance, is pronounced ['æktə ‖ 'æktɚ] with stress on the first syllable. While the first syllable contains the full vowel [æ], the (o) in the second syllable is not pronounced as [ɔː], [əʊ] or [ɒ], but it is reduced to schwa.

Function words have a special status when it comes to vowel reductions. While content words (nouns, verbs, adjectives and adverbs) express the subject matter of a sentence, function words (all other word classes) carry grammatical meaning and hold the sentence together. Because a speaker stresses words that are of communicative importance, function words are almost never stressed. Therefore, function words possess a weak form, in which the vowel is reduced. This weak form is not the exception but the rule for function words and will occur in the majority of cases. The strong form with a full vowel occurs only in few positions.

The concept of weak forms is best illustrated with the indefinite article (a). The strong form of ⟨a⟩ is [eɪ]. It will be very rare that speakers pronounce ⟨a⟩ in its strong form, as it only occurs when it is stressed, for example, in a sentence like: "*I didn't want your watch, I wanted a watch.*" In the majority of cases, however, the indefinite article will be pronounced [ə]. While for the indefinite article, it is the weak form that is taught at school, it might be surprising at first to which extent other function words can be reduced in their weak form.

Determiners	*a*	*an*	*the*		*his*	*her*	*your*	*some*
strong	[eɪ]	[æn]	[ði:]		[hɪz]	[hɔ:] / [hɜ˞:]	[jɔ:] / [jʊr]	[sʌm]
weak	[ə]	[ən]	[ðə] + conson. [ði] + vowel		[(h)ɪz]	[(h)ə] / [(h)ə˞]	[jə] / [jə˞]	[səm]

Pronouns	*he*	*she*	*you*	*me*	*him*	*us*	*them*	*who*
strong	[hi:]	[ʃi:]	[ju:]	[mi:]	[hɪm]	[ʌs]	[ðɛm]	[hu:]
weak	[hi]	[ʃi]	[ju]	[mi]	[(h)ɪm]	[əs]	[ðəm]	[hu]

Conj./Adverbs	*and*	*but*	*as*	*because*	*than*	*that*	*there*
strong	[ænd]	[bʌt]	[æz]	[bɪ'kɒz] / [bɪ'kʌz]	[ðæn]	[ðæt]	[ðɛə] / [ðɛr]
weak	[ən(d)]	[bət]	[əz]	[bɪ'kəz]	[ðən]	[ðət]	[ðə] / [ðə˞]

Prepositions	*at*	*for*	*from*	*of*	*to*
strong	[æt]	[fɔ:] / [fɔ:r]	[frɒm] / [frʌm]	[ɒv] / [ʌv]	[tu:]
weak	[ət]	[fə] / [fə˞]	[frəm]	[əv]	[tə] + conson. [tu] + vowel

Operators	*am*	*are*	*is*	*was*	*were*	*has*	*have*	*had*
strong	[æm]	[ɑː] [ɑːr]	[ɪz]	[wɒz] [wʌz]	[wɜː] [wɝː]	[hæz]	[hæv]	[hæd]
weak	[əm]	[ə] [ɚ]	[s, z]	[wəz]	[wə] [wɚ]	[(h)əz]	[(h)əv]	[(h)əd]

Operators	*do*	*does*	*can*	*will*	*shall*	*would*	*should*
strong	[duː]	[dʌz]	[kæn]	[wɪl]	[ʃæl]	[wʊd]	[ʃʊd]
weak	[dʊ,d(ə)]	[d(ə)z]	[kən]	[(w)əl]	[ʃəl]	[(w)əd]	[ʃ(ə)d]

Table 20: weak and strong forms of function words (RP top, GA bottom)

Strong forms of function words only occur in very restricted positions. In the majority of cases, however, a weak form is used. Strong forms occur whenever the word is stressed, as in the following cases:

- on its own: *"Who?"* [huː]
- at the end of a sentence or clause: *"Who is it for?"* [fɔː ‖ fɔːr]
- when emphasised: *"It is for her, not for him."* [hɜː ‖ hɝː], [hɪm]
- when joined by and/or: *"He was and is the best."* [wɒz ‖ wʌz], [ɪz]

Exercises

4.1

Transcribe the vowels in the following words. Note that the vowel letters correspond to a different vowel sound in each case.

(u)	use	put	cut
	burn	cure	sure
(a)	make	mad	far
	warn	want	many
(o)	code	job	short
	come	word	move
(e)	well	be	they
	here	there	were
(i)	time	give	stir

4.2

Which is the correct IPA symbol for the vowel in bold print?

love	[ɔː]	[ɒ]	[ʌ]	[ɑː]
watch	[ʌ]	[ɒ]	[ɑː]	[ɔː]
worm	[ɔː]	[ɜː]	[əʊ]	[ɝː]
guilty	[ʊ]	[uː]	[ɪ]	[wɪ]
appear	[ɪ]	[ɪə]	[iː]	[e]
industry	[ə]	[ʊ]	[ʌ]	[ɒ]
friend	[ɛ]	[iː]	[ɪ]	[eɪ]
sausage	[aʊ]	[ɔː]	[ɑː]	[ɒ]

4.3

Transcribe the following passage from *The War of the Worlds* by H. G. Wells, using weak forms where applicable.

After the glimpse I had had of the Martians emerging from the cylinder in which they had come to the earth from their planet, a kind of fascination paralysed my actions. I did not dare to go back towards the pit, but I felt a passionate longing to peer into it. I began walking, therefore, in a big curve, seeking some point of vantage and continually looking at the sand heaps that hid these new-comers to our earth. Once a leash of thin black whips, like the arms of an octopus, flashed across the sunset and was immediately withdrawn, and afterwards a thin rod rose up, joint by joint, bearing at its apex a circular disk that spun with a wobbling motion.

Listen to a recording of the transcription text online at:
www.phonetiker.net/transcript/

5 Acoustic Phonetics
[əˈkuːstɪk fəˈnɛtɪks]

Intensity

Intensity measures the loudness of a speech sound. When more air is exhaled within shorter time, the vocal folds vibrate with higher amplitude. Therefore, the sound becomes louder.

Loudness is generally measured in dB, a logarithmic scale modelled on human hearing. 0 dB is the threshold of hearing (at 1000 Hz): sounds more silent than this are not audible to humans. At about 120 dB lies the threshold of pain, meaning the pressure of sounds with such intensity would lead to permanent damage to the eardrum. When speaking, humans produce sounds of about 50-60 dB. (It is difficult to give a precise value, as the distance between mouth and measuring device has to be taken into consideration.)

Towards the end of an utterance, a phenomenon called declension occurs: the speech becomes less loud, as the lungs empty progressively and hence the pressure falls.

Pitch

Pitch means how high or low a tone is heard. The pitch of speech sounds depends on how fast or slow the vocal folds vibrate: if the frequency of their vibration is higher, i.e. if they vibrate faster, pitch is higher.

Frequency is most commonly measured in Hertz (Hz), which is cycles per second. So for a tone with a frequency of 100 Hz, the vocal folds open and close one hundred times in one second.

The anatomy of the larynx has a high impact on pitch. For instance, the larynx of a boy grows during puberty, so that also the vocal folds become longer. As they are longer, it takes them longer to open and close and therefore the tone they produce is lower. While men's vocal folds have a length of about 17-24 mm and vibrate at 120 Hz mean frequency, the vocal folds of women measure 13-17 mm and produce a mean frequency of 230 Hz. Babies, who have a very small larynx, produce a voice tone with a mean frequency of 400 Hz, as their vocal folds are only 5 mm long.

The vocal range of the human voice encompasses up to two octaves. While the whole range is used for singing, the speaking process only makes use of the lower half.

To produce a higher or lower tone, the muscular tension within the vocal folds is modified. By tilting the thyroid cartilage (upper part of the larynx) against the cricoid cartilage (lower ring of the larynx), the vocal folds can be stiffened and will become longer and leaner. In this case, the frequency becomes higher. Shorter, laxer and broader vocals folds, on the other hand, will produce a lower tone.

	vocal range
men	80 (bass) to 700 Hz
women	140 to 1100 Hz (coloratura soprano)
babies	100 to 1200 Hz

Table 21: vocal range of human voices

Formants

The fundamental frequency (f_0) is the frequency with which the vocal folds are set into vibration, i.e. how often per second the glottis opens and closes. However, the tone produced inside the larynx still needs to pass through the entire pharynx, oral and nasal cavity. These cavities act like a filter upon the tone.

Resonance describes the phenomenon by which the vibrations of one object can cause other objects to vibrate, such as an opera singer trying to get a wine glass to vibrate and eventually smash. A key factor is the natural frequency ("Eigenfrequenz") of an object. Only if the tone meets the natural frequency of the object, will resonance occur and the other object start to vibrate.

The same principle applies to the speech organs: when the tone produced by the vocal folds passes through pharynx, mouth and nose, frequencies that meet the natural frequencies of these cavities become amplified, while other frequencies are swallowed. The frequency bands that become amplified are always multiples of the fundamental frequency and are called formants.

In the articulation of different vowels, the tongue is in a different position each time. Consequently, the cavities above the larynx are differently shaped for different vowels, so that each vowel also has different, characteristic formants. It is in fact these formants that allow the ear to distinguish between different vowels.

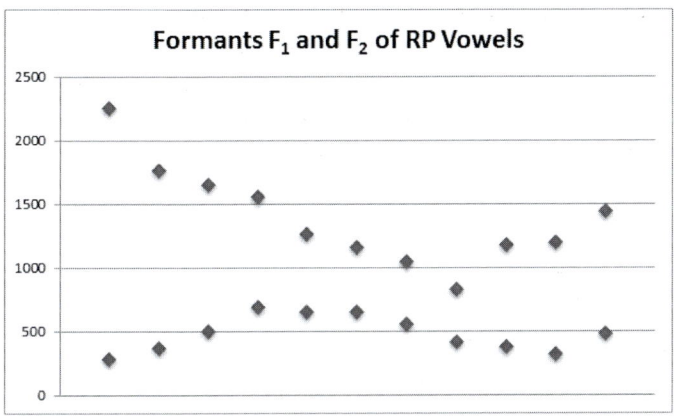

Left to right: [iː ɪ ɛ æ ʌ ɑː ɒ ɔː ʊ uː ɜː]

Figure 15: average formants of male BBC broadcasters in Hertz (Deterding 1997)

Noises and Tones

Depending on how a speech sound is produced, it possesses different acoustic qualities. Sounds can be classified as tones, noises or mixed sounds that have properties of both.

The main characteristic of tone sounds is a periodic wave pattern, similar to a sinus curve, that results from the vibration of the vocal folds. Tone sounds have pitch, which can be calculated by measuring the time from one peak in the sinus pattern to the next peak. Vowels are pure tone sounds.

Noise sounds, on the other hand, do not have a periodic wave representation and their sound results from the constriction in the oral cavity that causes friction or plosive release noises. A noise can best be imagined as the static sound a TV makes when there is no signal. Voiceless consonants, such as [f s ʃ], are pure noises.

Mixed sounds possess the acoustic properties of both tones and noises. In language, voiced consonants such as [v z ʒ] belong to this group. They have tone qualities, as the vocal folds vibrate, but also noise qualities from the constrictions in the oral cavity.

61

Reading Spectrograms

A spectrogram makes the physical composition of a speech signal visible. All the acoustic properties described above can be seen. Hence it is possible to identify individual sounds according to their sound class.

The figure below shows an oscillogram at the top and a spectrogram underneath. Already the oscillogram reveals information about a sound. The sine wave of tones can be seen, whereas noises show a black scribble. A sound is louder if the amplitude of the wave is higher. Pitch is higher when the sinus curves move closer together, lower when they are spaced further apart.

The spectrogram visualises the properties of sounds in more detail. It can be regarded as a three-dimensional coordinate system. The x-axis gives the utterance as it is spoken. The y-axis displays frequency starting with low pitch at about 70 Hz at the bottom and high pitch with several thousand Hertz at the top. The third dimension is intensity visualised through shades of grey. The darker an area, the louder is this specific frequency. White areas are silence.

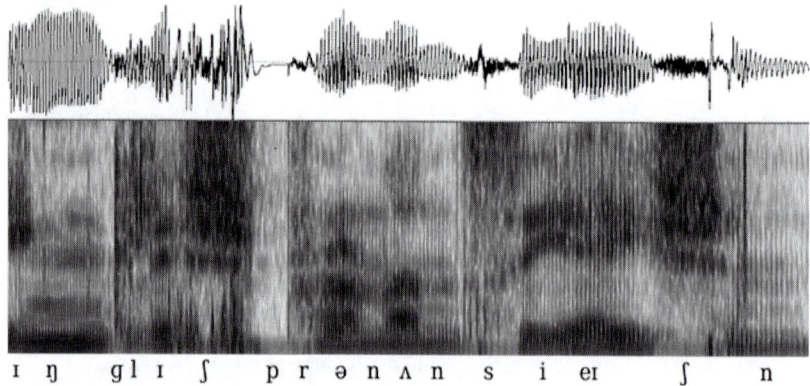

ɪ ŋ   gl ɪ ʃ   p r ə n ʌ n   s   i eɪ   ʃ   n

Figure 16: sample spectrogram and oscillogram

A first characteristic which can be observed in a spectrogram is whether a sound is voiced or voiceless. For voiced sounds including vowels, a black bar runs across at the bottom of the spectrogram ("voice bar"). This is missing for voiceless sounds. In vowel sounds, the formants become visible as several black bars running parallel to the voice bar. The position of the formants is different for different vowels. In diphthongs, the glide of the tongue can be observed as a change in the formants.

Also noise characteristics can be deciphered in a spectrogram. The friction noise of fricatives has a high concentration of energy in high frequencies (especially strong for [s z ʃ ʒ]), leading to dark-shaded areas at the top of the spectrogram. Plosives can be identified by the silence of the occlusion phase, which is white in the spectrogram, and the following burst of the explosion that leaves a narrow vertical black stripe.

Exercises

5.1

Find the corresponding spectrogram and oscillogram to the following names: *Angelina Jolie, Hugh Jackman, Nicole Kidman, James McAvoy.*

a)

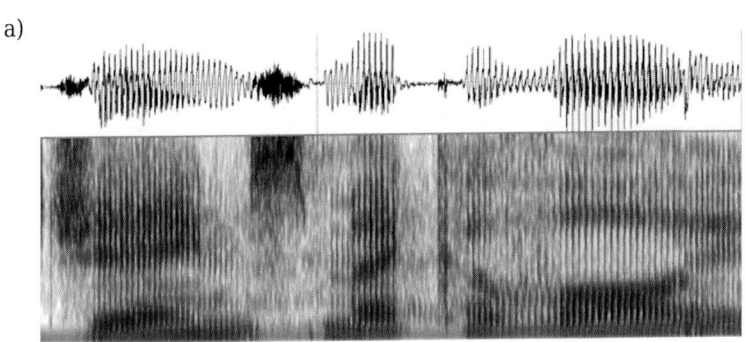

b)

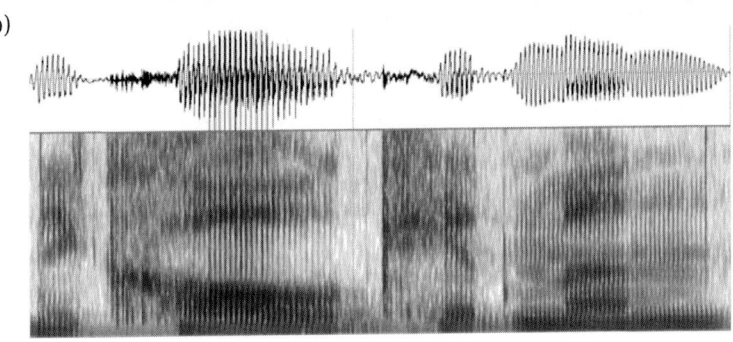

c)

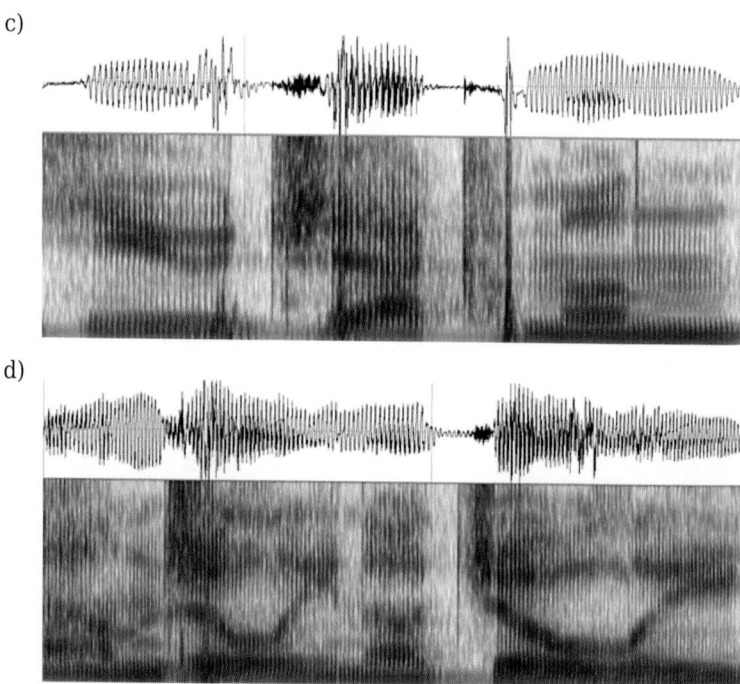

d)

5.2

Try singing an [ɑː] and go up and down with your voice. Now try the same with [s]. Why is this not possible?

5.3

Which transcription is correct?

	A	**B**	**C**
enough	[ə'nʌf]	[ə'nɑf]	[ɛ'nʌf]
throw	[θroʊ̯]	[θrəʊ̯]	[θrəʊ̯w]
meant	[mɛnt]	[mænt]	[mənt]
research	[ri'sɜːtʃ]	[ri'sɜːrtʃ]	['risɜ˞ːtʃ]
imagine	[i'mædʒɪn]	[ɪ'mædʒɪn]	[ɪ'mædʒən]
care	[kɛə̯]	[kɛr]	[kær]
freedom	['friːdɔːm]	['friːdɒm]	['friːdəm]
certain	['sɜ˞ːtən]	['sɜːtei̯n]	['sɜːtən]
closer	['kləʊ̯sə]	['kləʊ̯zə]	['kloʊ̯sə˞]
already	[ɑːl'rɛdi]	[ɔːl'rɛdi]	[ɒl'rɛdi]
return	[ri'tɜːn]	[rə'tɜːn]	[ri'tɜ˞ːn]
actually	['æktʃəli]	['æktʃʊli]	['æktʃɛli]
year	[jiːr]	[jɪr]	[jɪə̯]
entire	[ɪn'tai̯r]	[ɪn'tai̯ə]	[ɛn'tai̯ə]
whole	[huːl]	[hoʊ̯l]	[həʊ̯l]
love	[lɒf]	[lʌv]	[lɒv]

5.4

Transcribe the following passage from *Peter Pan* by J. M. Barrie.

Feeling that Peter was on his way back, the Neverland had again woke into life. We ought to use the pluperfect and say wakened, but woke is better and was always used by Peter. In his absence things are usually quiet on the island. The fairies take an hour longer in the morning, the beasts attend to their young, the redskins feed heavily for six days and nights, and when pirates and lost boys meet they merely bite their thumbs at each other. But with the coming of Peter, who hates lethargy, they are under way again: if you put your ear to the ground now, you would hear the whole island seething with life.

 Listen to a recording of the transcription text online at: www.phonetiker.net/transcript/

6 Allophonic Variation
[ælə'fɒnɪk vɛəri'eɪʃn̩]

Speech sounds differ in accordance with the speech organs that are involved in their articulation. The main criteria for consonants are manner of articulation (plosive, fricative, …) and place of articulation (bilabial, alveolar, velar, …) as well as tension (fortis/lenis) and voice (voiceless/voiced). For vowels, the part of tongue (front/central/back) and height of tongue (high, mid, low, …) play a role as well as lip-rounding (rounded/unrounded) and length (long/short).

In connected speech, however, the speech organs do not neatly articulate one phone after another. Rather, the speech organs are in constant motion. In this process of moving from one articulatory position to the next, often one movement is not carried out completely or skipped entirely. The articulation of a sound is hence influenced by the sound that precedes or follows it. Therefore sounds often exhibit different articulatory properties that diverge from their normal, canonical realisation. These variants of a speech sound are called allophones.

The fact that a sound is influenced by the sounds that surround it is referred to as co-articulation. Most often the result of co-articulation is assimilation: one sound becomes more similar to its neighbour. The feature that is assimilated can be any of the criteria of articulation: manner and place of articulation or voice for consonants, part and height of tongue as well as lip-rounding and length for vowels.

Place of Articulation: Advanced or Retracted

Consonants in connected speech are often articulated with a different place of articulation than when pronounced in isolation. Their actual place is either further to the front (advanced) or further to the back (retracted) of the mouth. The IPA provides several possibilities for the transcription of such divergent articulations. In some cases, there is an extra symbol, such as for a labiodental nasal [ɱ]. For some positions, the place of articulation can be specified with the help of a diacritic. "Dental", for instance, can be transcribed with a subscript [◌̪] below the sound in question. If no dedicated diacritic is available for the place of articulation, it can be specified as advanced with a subscript plus [◌̟] or as retracted with a subscript minus [◌̠].

The phoneme inventory of English consonants shows that plosives and nasals occur at three different positions only: bilabial, alveolar and velar. In connected speech, however, the place of articulation is often assimilated to the following sound (regressive assimilation). Therefore, the three phonemes /p/, /t/ and /k/ show in fact allophonic variants at almost all positions.

The alveolar consonants [t], [d] and [n] are articulated with the tip of the tongue in direct contact with the alveolar ridge. When saying the words ⟨tie⟩ or ⟨no⟩, the contact of the tongue with the roof of the mouth before the vowel can be felt. In contrast to this canonical realisation of /t/ and /n/, the place of contact between tongue and upper articulators is different in the words ⟨month⟩, where it is further front, and ⟨try⟩, where it is further back.

In words such as ⟨month⟩, ⟨tenth⟩ or ⟨eighth⟩, the place of articulation is dental. Even though these words also contain /t/ or /n/, the position of the tongue is not at the alveolar ridge, but further towards the front, at the teeth. The reason is the following [θ], which is dental. So instead of first moving to the alveolar ridge to then move on to the teeth, one movement is economised and the tip of the tongue moves directly to the teeth for the articulation of /t/. Hence, the realisation of the phonemes /t/ and /n/ is not alveolar in these cases, but dental: [t̪] and [n̪].

Dental [t̪] or [n̪] are [t] and [n] advanced from the alveolar ridge, but it is equally possible that alveolar sounds are retracted. In words, such as ⟨try⟩ where [t] is followed by [r], which is post-alveolar, the articulation of [t] is also transferred to that region. When comparing the position where the tongue touches the roof of the mouth, this position is much farther back for ⟨try⟩ than it is for ⟨tie⟩, for example.

The velar sounds /k/ and /g/ also have different allophonic realisations. This becomes apparent when listening carefully to the [k] sound in the words ⟨key⟩ [kiː] and ⟨car⟩ [kɑː ‖ kɑːr]. The sound in ⟨key⟩ sounds somehow brighter and higher pitched, while in ⟨car⟩ it is darker and more muffled. The reason for this difference is that the [k] in ⟨key⟩ is not truly velar. Before front high vowels, such as [iː], velar sounds are articulated more advanced: they are pre-velar.

While bilabial sounds cannot possibly be advanced, there are allophones of bilabial plosives and nasals that are retracted to a labiodental position. A labiodental nasal can be heard in the English word ⟨comfort⟩ [ˈkʌɱfət ‖ ˈkʌɱfɚt]. The place of articulation is that of the following sound: [f] is labiodental and so the preceding nasal is regressively assimilated to that position. The same sound can be heard in the German word ⟨Senf⟩ [zɛɱf]. While German speakers hear that they somehow pronounce an [m] in ⟨Senf⟩ and not an [n], it is, in fact neither, but a labiodental nasal.

Also normally bilabial plosives are produced with a labiodental closing in connected speech. Examples are words such as ⟨obvious⟩ ['ɒḇviəs ‖ 'ɑːḇviəs] or ⟨cupful⟩ ['kʌpfʊl], in which a bilabial plosive precedes a labiodental fricative. For [b] and [p], it is not both lips that touch, but the lower lip touching the upper teeth.

	advanced	retracted
alveolar plosives /t/, /d/	dental *eighth* [eɪt̪θ] *width* [wɪd̪θ]	post-alveolar *try* [t̠raɪ] *drive* [d̠raɪv]
alveolar nasal/lateral /n/, /l/	dental *month* [mʌn̪θ] *health* [hɛl̪θ]	—
bilabial plosives /p/, /b/	—	labiodental *obvious* ['ɒḇviəs] *cupful* ['kʌpfʊl]
bilabial nasal /m/	—	labiodental *comfort* ['kʌɱfət] *pamphlet* ['pæɱflɪt]
velar plosives /k/, /g/	pre-velar *key* [k̟iː] *geese* [g̟iːs]	—

Table 22: advanced and retracted articulations

Secondary Articulations

Allophones can occur as a result of secondary articulations. Here, it is not the place of articulation that is assimilated as such. Rather, an articulatory feature occurs that is needed for an adjacent sound but would not be part of the articulation of the present sound if pronounced in isolation.

Lip-rounding before rounded vowels is an example of a secondary articulation in English. In the word ⟨two⟩ [tuː], the vowel [uː] is a rounded, back, high vowel. Therefore, the lips need to be rounded for its articulation. However, lip-rounding does not set in after the /t/ as could be expected, but before the word. /t/ is produced as an alveolar plosive but with rounded lips (transcribed as [tʷ]) which is not a feature of the canonical realisation found in ⟨tip⟩. The same phenomenon can also be observed in ⟨who⟩ [hʷuː], ⟨soon⟩ [sʷuːn] or in ⟨shoot⟩ [ʃʷuːt], for example.

The dark [ɫ] is another example for a secondary articulation. In the articulation of clear [l], the tip of the tongue lies at the alveolar ridge and the sides of the tongue are pulled downwards. For dark [ɫ], the articulation is the same, but additionally the back of the tongue is raised towards the velum.

Manner of Articulation: Difference in Release

All plosives have three phases: obstruction, occlusion and release. In connected speech, regressive assimilation can be observed which affects the release phase: the speech organs move into the position for the following speech sound too early so that a feature of that sound can already be heard in the release of the plosive.

Nasal release occurs before syllabic nasals with the same place of articulation as the plosive (homorganic). The explosion that occurs in the release phase goes through the nasal cavity. ⟨button⟩ [ˈbʌtn̩], ⟨sudden⟩ [ˈsʌdn̩] or German ⟨Lappen⟩ [ˈlapm̩] are words where a nasal release can be observed. For ⟨button⟩, as an example, the following articulatory movements could be expected for the sound sequence of plosive plus nasal: during the occlusion phase, the tip of the tongue rests at the alveolar ridge. For the release phase, it should move away, allowing the accumulated air to escape. Finally, the tip of the tongue should move back to the alveolar ridge for [n], while simultaneously the velum is lowered in the back of the mouth, opening the nasal passage. However, most speakers will omit one movement and keep the tip of the tongue at the alveolar ridge the whole time and only lower the velum in the release of [t]. Pronounced this way, the air accumulated in the occlusion phase passes through the nose. Plosives with nasal release are transcribed as [pⁿ tⁿ kⁿ bⁿ dⁿ gⁿ].

A lateral release can be observed for [t] and [d] before syllabic [l̩], for example in ⟨bottle⟩ [ˈbɒtl̩ ‖ ˈbɑːtl̩]. The lowering of the sides of the tongue for [l] that makes the airstream flow sideways around the tongue can already be heard in the release of the plosive. Similarly to the nasal release, both [t d] and [l] are homorganic, so that the tip of the tongue as articulating organ would need to move away from the alveolar ridge for the release of the plosive and then move back to that position for the lateral [l]. And similarly to the nasal release, it is exactly this movement that speakers leave out. In the transition from [t d] to [l], the tip of the tongue remains in place and only the sides of the tongue are lowered at the release of the plosive, which is needed for the lateral [l]. Hence, the accumulated air escapes in the release of the plosive laterally at the sides of the tongue. Laterally released plosives are transcribed [tˡ dˡ].

When the same plosive occurs twice successively, only the second plosive is released. In the example ⟨biscuit tin⟩ it can be observed that the [t] of ⟨biscuit⟩ is pronounced without the typical explosion noise we hear when pronouncing the word in isolation ['bɪskɪt]. The [t] is not completely missing, however: people do not say ['bɪskɪ tɪn]. What is missing is the release phase of the first [t]. After the approach and occlusion phase, the second [t] starts right away and only this one is audibly released: ['bɪskɪt̚ tɪn].

The same phenomenon can be observed when the following consonant is not the same plosive, but a consonant which has the same place of articulation. So for instance, [t] can be unreleased before other alveolar sounds, such as [n] or [l].

Also at the end of an utterance, plosives occur often unreleased. The articulation of the plosive remains incomplete: people stop speaking before the plosive is finished.

nasal release before syllabic, homorganic nasals	*button* ['bʌt^{n}n̩] *sudden* ['sʌd^{n}n̩]
lateral release before syllabic, homorganic laterals	*bottle* ['bɒtˡl̩] ‖ 'bɑːtˡl̩] *battle* ['bætˡl̩]
no release before homorganic consonants and at the end of a phrase	*blackcurrant* [blæk̚'kʌrənt] *witness* ['wɪt̚nəs] *that lift* [ðət̚ 'lɪft]

Table 23: different releases of plosives

Aspiration and De-Voicing

Aspiration occurs regularly for fortis plosives at the beginning of a syllable. Native speakers of English or German are usually not aware of it, but the /p/ in words such as ⟨span⟩ [spæn], ⟨pan⟩ [pæn] and ⟨nap⟩ [næp] sound different. While the /p/ in ⟨pan⟩ is aspirated (transcribed as [pʰ]), the /p/ in ⟨span⟩ or ⟨nap⟩ is not. The explosion of the [pʰ] in ⟨pan⟩ sounds more powerful than in the unaspirated realisation [p]. How much an English or German native speaker makes use of aspiration for fortis plosives at the beginning of syllables becomes apparent when listening to languages that do not have aspiration, such as French or Russian. When Frenchmen say ⟨Paris⟩ in French, it sounds almost like they pronounce a /b/, simply because fortis plosives are not aspirated in French.

The question of aspiration is related to voicing. For voiced sounds, the vocal folds vibrate, while for voiceless sounds they do not. Setting the vocal folds into vibration for voiced sounds such as [z] or [w] is not a problem. The case is different for plosives, where the air stream is stopped for the occlusion phase of the plosive, so that the vocal folds cannot possibly continue to vibrate at full intensity. Therefore, for plosives, the question is not so much whether or not the vocal folds vibrate, but rather how quickly they can resume full vibration after the release phase of the plosive. The time between the release of the plosive and the setting in of voice is called Voice Onset Time (VOT). Voiced plosives have a negative VOT: the vibration of the vocal folds starts again before the plosive is released. In the articulation of voiceless plosives, voice sets in a few milliseconds after the release. For aspirated plosives, this time is considerably longer: in English about 30 milliseconds.

Normally, tension and voice correlate: fortis consonants are voiceless, while lenis consonants are voiced. In connected speech, however, lenis consonants can become devoiced when they are adjacent to voiceless sounds or silence (which after all is also voiceless). That is why it makes sense to specify both tension and voice in the description of consonants, since in connected speech devoiced lenis consonants exist. The muscular effort in their articulation is not increased, so that they remain lenis. However, the vibration of the vocal folds stops too early or does not start early enough, so that they are in fact voiceless. Lenis plosives, fricatives and affricates become voiceless before other voiceless sounds or silence. Approximants including [l] become voiceless after aspirated plosives.

aspiration	fortis plosives	[pʰ tʰ kʰ]
	syllable initially, before silence	*team* [tʰiːm]
de-voicing	lenis obstruents	[b̥ d̥ g̊ ɣ̥ z̥ ʒ̊ d̥ʒ̊]
	before voiceless consonants	*has to* [hæz̥ tu]
	approximants	[l̥ ɹ̥ j̊ w̥]
	after aspirated plosives	*please* [pʰl̥iːz]

Table 24: aspiration and devoicing

Length

Length is one criterion in the classification of monophthongs, but also the length of a sound is influenced by the surrounding sounds as a result of co-articulation. Depending on the voice of the following consonant, a vowel appears shorter when it is followed by a voiceless consonant and longer when it is followed by a voiced consonant.

If we compare the two words ⟨bad⟩ and ⟨bat⟩, we will find that both contain the same short higher low front vowel. Upon closer observation, however, the [æ] in ⟨bad⟩ seems to be longer than the [æ] in ⟨bat⟩. It still remains a short vowel, but there is a difference in length between the two realisations.

The same phenomenon can be observed for long monophthongs: the vowel seems to be shorter when followed by a voiceless consonant. An example is ⟨bead⟩ and ⟨beat⟩. Both contain a long high front vowel, yet in ⟨beat⟩ the [iː] does not seem to be as long as in ⟨bead⟩.

	before lenis consonant	**before fortis consonant**
short vowels	*lid* [lɪ·d]	*lit* [lɪt]
	bad [bæ·d]	*bat* [bæt]
	buzz [bʌ·z]	*bus* [bʌs]
long vowels	*bead* [biːd]	*beat* [bi·t]
	shoed [ʃuːd]	*shoot* [ʃu·t]
	starve [stɑːv]	*staff* [stɑ·f]

Table 25: lengthening and shortening of monophthongs

This difference in length can be explained by co-articulation during which the following sound is anticipated. If the vibration of the vocal folds continues into the next consonant (or is interrupted only shortly for the occlusion phase of the plosive), the vowel is stretched. If, on the other hand, the vibration of the vocal folds must stop for a following voiceless consonant, it leads to a shorter articulation of the vowel.

Narrow vs. Broad Transcription

All these different realisations of consonants and vowels can be transcribed with the help of IPA. A narrow transcription can note all these phenomena, while in a broad transcription they are ignored. The question of how much or how little should be transcribed depends on what the transcription is for and also what function the individual sounds have in a language. In other words, whether a sound is a phoneme or an allophone.

Narrow transcription becomes important, when the goal of transcription is not so much the standard pronunciation of a word, but how individual speakers pronounce a word, for instance when investigating accents and dialects.

Exercises

6.1

The table gives the place of articulation for the sound in isolation. What place of articulation does the sound have in the following words?

/d/	alveolar [d]	*d*rag	post-alveolar [ɖ]
/n/	alveolar [n]	*labyrinth*	
/m/	bilabial [m]	*sym*phony	
/t/	alveolar [t]	*t*ool	
/k/	velar [k]	*k*eep	

6.2

Which transcription is correct?

	A	B	C
perfect	[ˈpɝːfɪkt]	[ˈpɜːfɛkt]	[ˈpɜːfɪkt]
collect	[kəˈlɛkt]	[kɒˈlɛkt]	[kəˈlʌkt]
suppose	[səˈpɔːz]	[səˈpəʊ̯z]	[səˈpoʊ̯z]
country	[ˈkɒntri]	[ˈkaʊ̯ntri]	[ˈkʌntri]
project	[ˈprɒʤɛkt]	[ˈprəʊ̯ʤɛkt]	[ˈprɑːʤɛkt]
journey	[ˈʤɝːni]	[ˈʤɜːneɪ̯]	[ˈʤɜːni]
action	[ˈækʃn̩]	[ˈæktʃn̩]	[ˈæktʃn̩]
occur	[əˈkɝː]	[əˈkɜː]	[əˈkjʊə̯]
money	[ˈmʌni]	[ˈmɒni]	[ˈmʌneɪ̯]
gesture	[ˈgɛstʃə]	[ˈʤɛstʃə]	[ˈʤɛstʃɚ]
injure	[ˈɪnʤʊə̯]	[ˈɪnʤə]	[ˈɪnʤɚ]
language	[ˈlæŋgwæʤ]	[ˈlæŋgwəʤ]	[ˈlæŋgwɪʤ]
stranger	[ˈstreɪ̯nʒə]	[ˈstreɪ̯nʒə]	[ˈstreɪ̯nʤɚ]
stove	[stɔːv]	[stoʊ̯v]	[stəʊ̯v]
examine	[ɪgˈzæmɪn]	[ɪkˈsæmɪn]	[ɛkˈzæmɪn]
somebody	[ˈsʌmbɒdi]	[ˈsʌmbʌdi]	[ˈsʌmbədi]

6.3

Transcribe the following passage from *Journey to the Centre of the Earth* by Jules Vernes. Try to make a narrow transcription if you feel adventurous.

The cold in the shades of this singular forest was intense. For nearly an hour we wandered about in this visible darkness. At length I left the spot, and once more returned to the shores of the lake, to light and comparative warmth. But the amazing vegetation of subterraneous land was not confined to gigantic mushrooms. New wonders awaited us at every step. We had not gone many hundred yards, when we came upon a mighty group of other trees with discolored leaves.

 Listen to a recording of the transcription text online at: www.phonetiker.net/transcript/

6.4

Read the following IPA transcription from *Les Misérables* by Victor Hugo and write the text orthographically.

[wɛn fãti:n 'sɔ: ðət ʃi wəz meɪ̯kɪŋ hə 'lɪvɪŋ | ʃi fɛlt 'd͡ʒɔɪfəl fər ə məʊ̯mənt ‖ tə lɪv 'ɒnɪstli baɪ̯ hər əʊ̯n 'leɪ̯bə | wɒt 'mɜ:si frəm 'hɛvn̩ ‖ ðə teɪ̯st fə 'wɜ:k həd rɪə̯li rɪ't͡ɜ:nd tə hɜ: ‖ ʃi bɔ:t ə 'lʊkɪŋ gla:s | tʊk 'plɛʒər ɪn səveɪ̯ɪŋ ɪn 'ɪt hə 'ju:θ | hə bju:təfl̩ 'hɛə̯ | hə faɪ̯n 'ti:θ | ʃi fə'gɒt mɛni θɪŋz]

[wɛn fãti:n 'sɔ: ðət ʃi wəz meɪ̯kɪŋ hɚ 'lɪvɪŋ | ʃi fɛlt 'd͡ʒɔɪfəl fɚ ə moʊ̯mənt ‖ tə lɪv 'ɑ:nəstli baɪ̯ hɚ oʊ̯n 'leɪ̯bɚ | wʌt 'mɜ˞:si frəm 'hɛvn̩ ‖ ðə teɪ̯st fɚ 'wɜ˞:k həd ri:li rɪ't͡ɜ˞:nd tə hɜ˞: ‖ ʃi bɔ:t ə 'lʊkɪŋ glæs | tʊk 'plɛʒɚ ɪn səveɪ̯ɪŋ ɪn 'ɪt hɚ 'ju:θ | hɚ bju:təfl̩ 'hɛr | hɚ faɪ̯n 'ti:θ | ʃi fɚ'gɑ:t mɛni θɪŋz]

 Listen to a recording of the transcription text online at: www.phonetiker.net/transcript/

7 Phonemes and Allophones
['fəʊniːmz ənd 'æləfəʊnz]

A sound is considered a phone when it is part of the speech process. Hence, other sounds that humans are capable of producing, such as belching, humming or whistling, do not count as phones. Phones are ultimately combined to communicate meaningful words. It is not the sounds themselves that carry meaning, but only their combination leads to meaningful units. In this process, not all sounds found in a language have the same function.

Imagine English was an exotic, unknown language. We do not know a single word of this language, neither the spelling nor sound system. Our aim is now to investigate this language and hopefully comprehend it someday. Therefore we talk to people, even though we do not understand much at first. In these conversations, we hear the words [laɪt], [raɪt], [ɫaɪt], [ɾaɪt], [naɪt] and [faɪt] several times. All these words differ in one sound. The important question is now what the status of these sounds is. In other words, are the six words in our list really six different words?

Luckily, we do have a good knowledge of English and know that we are only dealing with four separate words. [ɫ] is the dark /l/, which occurs in Received Pronunciation except before vowels where the clear /l/ is heard, but in General American in all positions. So a British speaker would pronounce (light) as [laɪt] and an American speaker as [ɫaɪt]. The situation is similar for (right), which an RP speaker would pronounce [raɪt], a speaker from Scotland, however, with a tongue-tip R-sound similar to the one heard in Southern Germany: [ɾaɪt]. Therefore, the six sounds [l], [r], [ɫ], [ɾ], [n] and [f] do not have the same status in English.

While it is not important whether I say [laɪt] or [ɫaɪt] – I am still saying the same word, there is a considerable difference whether I talk about [laɪt] or [naɪt]. The sounds [l] and [n] are phonemes in English, meaning that although the sounds do not mean anything by themselves, they lead to a difference in meaning: [naɪt] is the opposite of day, [laɪt] is what is emitted from the sun. The same is not true for [l] and [ɫ], which do not establish a meaning contrast. Hence, [l] and [ɫ] are not phonemes in English, but rather variants of one and the same sound: they are both allophones of /l/.

A phonetic transcription is indicated by square brackets [ ] and can be quite precise or narrow and transcribe allophonic variants. In a phonemic transcription, on the other hand, sound differences are only transcribed if the sound is a phoneme in the specific language, i.e. if it fulfils a meaning-distinguishing function. To indicate that a sound has phonemic status, it is put between slant brackets / /.

phonetic	orthographic	phonemic
[laɪt] [ɫaɪt]	⟨light⟩	/laɪt/
[raɪt] [ɾaɪt]	⟨right⟩	/raɪt/
[naɪt]	⟨night⟩	/naɪt/
[faɪt]	⟨fight⟩	/faɪt/

Table 26: examples for phonemes and allophones

The difference between phonemes and allophones becomes apparent when considering the allophonic variation of plosives, for instance. In the previous chapter, it was shown that English does not only possess three different plosives, but that there are advanced and retracted articulations, so that plosives occur nearly at every place of articulation.

However, not all these different plosives have a function in English. The dental, alveolar and post-alveolar plosives are all variants of one and the same conceptual unit, the phoneme /t/. In other words, [t̪], [t] and [t̠] are allophones of /t/.

bilabial plosive	labio-dental plosive	dental plosive	alveolar plosive	post-alveolar plosive	pre-velar plosive	velar plosive
— *are allophones of phonemes* —						
↘	↗	↘	↓	↗	↘	↗
/p/		/t/			/k/	

Figure 17: relation between allophones and phonemes

Phonemes are abstract units. Therefore, it would be incorrect to say that a dental plosive is a variant of the alveolar plosive. Rather, alveolar and dental plosive together constitute one phoneme. As phonemes are abstract, they cannot be pronounced. What can be pronounced is an allophone from the wide range of allophones that one phoneme may possess. The abstract character of phonemes can be nicely illustrated with an example from the German language.

In German, the digraph (combination of two letters) ⟨ch⟩ corresponds to two different sounds: [ç] as in ⟨nicht⟩ and [x] as in ⟨Nacht⟩. Whether ⟨ch⟩ is pronounced as [ç] or [x] simply depends on the preceding vowel: if it is a front vowel, ⟨ch⟩ is pronounced [ç]; if it is a back vowel, it is pronounced [x]. Together, [ç] and [x] constitute one phoneme in German. Pronouncing this phoneme would be a difficult undertaking. What could only be done, is to choose one of the two allophones and pronounce this instead.

Minimal Pair Test

Whether a sound has phoneme status in a language can be determined with the Minimal Pair Test. A minimal pair consists of two words that differ in one sound and one sound only, regardless of their spelling. If a minimal pair exists for a phone, i.e. other words can be found that have a different sound in that position, then this sound has the status of a phoneme. In English, [s] is a phoneme and can therefore be transcribed as /s/, because [sɪt] contrasts with [fɪt] or [hɪt], [raɪs] means something entirely different than [raɪm] and [krʌst] is a different word than [krʌʃt].

If, on the other hand, no minimal pair can be found, the phones are allophones of another phoneme. For instance, in German, no minimal pairs exist where [ç] and [x] lead to differences in meaning. In English, no two words only differ in clear [l] and dark [ɫ].

	minimal pair?
cut and *cup*	Yes. [kʌt] and [kʌp]
cent and *sent*	No. Identical pronunciation (homophones): [sɛnt]
here and *there*	No. Contrasting in two sounds: [hɪə ‖ hɪr] and [ðɛə ‖ ðɛr]
live (verb/adj.)	Yes. [lɪv] and [laɪv]
tie and *eye*	No. No contrasting sound in one word: [taɪ] and [aɪ]
war and *door*	Yes. [wɔː ‖ wɔːr] and [dɔː ‖ dɔːr]

Table 27: examples for minimal pairs

Distribution of Allophones

Phonemes occur in parallel distribution. This means that they can be found in all positions within a word. /t/ can be found word-initially in ⟨tip⟩ [tɪp], in mid-position in ⟨written⟩ [ˈrɪtn̩] or word-finally in ⟨but⟩ [bʌt]. (Exceptions are /ŋ/ and /ʒ/ that only occurs at the end of a syllable and /h/ that only occurs at its beginning.)

Allophones, on the other hand, appear in complementary distribution. In a specific position, only one allophone will occur and it can be predicted which. An example is the aspiration of plosives in English. For instance, /p/ sounds differ in the words ⟨pin⟩, ⟨spin⟩ and ⟨tip⟩. While in ⟨pin⟩ /p/ is pronounced with an aspiration [pʰɪn], this aspiration is missing in [spɪn] and [tɪp]. This is no coincidence, as there is a rule that predicts in which position which allophone can be found: wherever /p/ occurs as the first sound in a syllable and is followed by a vowel or voiced consonant, it is realised as [pʰ], in all other positions [p] is heard.

Free variants are variations of one phoneme that are not restricted to a specific position. Some textbooks consider free variants as allophones, others as a separate category in their own right. An example for free variants is /r/, both in English and German. While RP and GA speakers pronounce ⟨read⟩ with an approximant [ɹiːd], Scottish English has an alveolar tap instead [riːd], some regions in the US a retroflex sound [ɻiːd]. In Standard German ⟨Ring⟩ is pronounced with a velar fricative transcribed as [ʁɪŋ]. However, many dialects, in Bavaria for example, use an alveolar tap for /r/ [rɪŋ].

Phonemic Status in Different Languages

Phonemes are language-specific. Every language possesses its own phonology, so that the question of whether a phone participates in the construction of meaning and is hence a phoneme or whether it does not and must be classified as an allophone, needs to be answered for each language individually.

The sound [ɪ], for example, is found both in English and in German. In these two languages, it contrasts with [iː]. It makes a difference whether I say ⟨fill⟩ [fɪl] or ⟨feel⟩ [fiːl] in English and ⟨Mitte⟩ [ˈmɪtə] or ⟨Miete⟩ [ˈmiːtə] in German. There is a clear difference in meaning between these two respective words. In Canadian French, the phone [ɪ] is also heard in words such as ⟨petite⟩

[ptɪt]. However, in contrast to English or German, if I pronounce this word [pti:t] with a long [i:], I have not said a different word. In French, [ɪ] and [i:] are not two different phonemes but simply variations of one and the same phoneme; they are allophones.

The sound [ç] is quite frequent in German. It is the consonant heard in ⟨ich⟩. In English, this sound is not non-existent, but it has a different status. It can be heard in English words, such as ⟨cute⟩ [kçu:t], ⟨tube⟩ [tçu:b] or ⟨human⟩ ['çu:mən]. However, the phonological status of this phone is a different one in the two languages. In German, [ç] contrasts with other sounds: in ⟨Kirche⟩ and ⟨Kirsche⟩ with [ʃ] or in ⟨welchen⟩ and ⟨welken⟩ with [k]. Therefore, it makes a difference in meaning whether I pronounce [ç] or a different phone. In English, on the other hand, the situation is different.

The word ⟨tube⟩ [tçu:b] is similar to words such as ⟨duke⟩ [dju:k], ⟨beauty⟩ ['bju:ti] or ⟨mute⟩ [mju:t]. In these words, we find [j] before the vowel, so that [ç] only seems to be the voiceless counterpart of [j]. Unlike in German, in English there are no two words where [ç] contrasts with another sound. Therefore, [ç] is an allophone of the phoneme /j/ in English.

$$\left.\begin{array}{l} [\,\varsigma\,] \\ \text{front vowels} \\[1em] [\,\times\,] \\ \text{back vowels} \end{array}\right\} \;\; /\times/$$

Exercises

7.1

Spot the mistake in the following transcriptions.

job	[jɒb]
bank	[bænk]
stronger	[ˈstrɒŋə]
sight	[sɑɪ̯t]
cutter	[ˈkʌttə]
company	[ˈkɒmpəni]
uninvited	[ʌnɪnˈvaɪ̯ted]

7.2

Try to find as many minimal pairs as possible for

    a)   consonants followed by [m]
    b)   vowels in-between [h] and [d]
    c)   consonants after [rɪ]

7.3

The TRAP words contain [æ] in both RP and GA, while the PALM words have [ɑː] in both varieties. The BATH words, on the other hand, have [ɑː] in RP and [æ] in GA. Sort the following words into these three categories.

after, almond, arrow, ask, bra, calm, chance, crash, demand, drama, father, glass, ham, last, laughter, mass, math, random, rather, sack, tap

7.4

Transcribe the following passage from *The Fall of the House of Usher* by Edgar A. Poe. Try to make a narrow transcription if you feel adventurous.

During the whole of a dull, dark, and soundless day in the autumn of the year, when the clouds hung oppressively low in the heavens, I had been passing alone, on horseback, through a singularly dreary tract of country; and at length found myself, as the shades of the evening drew on, within view of the melancholy House of Usher. I know not how it was – but, with the first glimpse of the building, a sense of insufferable gloom pervaded my spirit.

 Listen to a recording of the transcription text online at: www.phonetiker.net/transcript/

7.5

Read the following IPA transcription from *Jane Eyre* by Charlotte Brontë and write the text orthographically.

[ɪt wəz vɛri ˈnɪə̯ | bət nɒt jɛt ɪn ˈsaɪ̯t | wɛn | ɪn ədɪʃn̩ tə ðə ˈtræmp ˈtræmp | aɪ̯ hɜːd ə ˈrʌʃ ʌndə ðə ˈhɛdʒ | ənd kləʊ̯s daʊ̯n baɪ̯ ðə ˈheɪ̯zl̩ stɛmz | glaɪ̯dɪd ə greɪ̯t ˈdɒg | huːz blæk ənd waɪ̯t ˈkʌlə | meɪ̯d hɪm ə dɪstɪŋkt ˈɒbdʒɛkt əgɛnst ðə ˈtriːz ‖ ðə ˈdɒg keɪ̯m baʊ̯ndɪŋ ˈbæk | ənd siːŋ hɪz ˈmɑːstər ɪn ə priˈdɪkəmənt | ənd ˈhɪə̯rɪŋ ðə hɔːs ˈgrəʊ̯n | ˈbɑːkt tɪl ði ˈiːvnɪŋ hɪlz ˈɛkəʊ̯d ðə saʊ̯nd | wɪtʃ wəz ˈdiːp ɪn prəpɔːʃn̩ tə hɪz ˈmægnɪtjuːd]

[ɪt wəz vɛri ˈnɪr | bət nɑːt jɛt ɪn ˈsaɪ̯t | wɛn | ɪn ədɪʃn̩ tə ðə ˈtræmp ˈtræmp | aɪ̯ hɜ˞ːd ə ˈrʌʃ ʌndɚ ðə ˈhɛdʒ | ənd kloʊ̯s daʊ̯n baɪ̯ ðə ˈheɪ̯zl̩ stɛmz | glaɪ̯dɪd ə greɪ̯t ˈdɔːg | huːz blæk ənd waɪ̯t ˈkʌlɚ | meɪ̯d hɪm ə dɪstɪŋkt ˈɑːbdʒɛkt əgɛnst ðə ˈtriːz ‖ ðə ˈdɔːg keɪ̯m baʊ̯ndɪŋ ˈbæk | ənd siːŋ hɪz ˈmæstɚ ɪn ə priˈdɪkəmənt | ənd ˈhɪrɪŋ ðə hɔːrs ˈgroʊ̯n | ˈbɑːrkt tɪl ði ˈiːvnɪŋ hɪlz ˈɛkoʊ̯d ðə saʊ̯nd | wɪtʃ wəz ˈdiːp ɪn prəpɔːrʃn̩ tə hɪz ˈmægnɪtuːd]

 Listen to a recording of the transcription text online at: www.phonetiker.net/transcript/

8 Phonological Processes
[fəʊ̯nə'lɒdʒɪkəl 'prəʊ̯sɛsɪz]

All speech is subject to co-articulation. In connected speech, the speech organs are in constant motion and the individual sounds are not pronounced with the articulation found in isolation, as neighbouring sounds influence each other. The result of this process can be an allophonic variant, but also an entirely different phoneme.

Assimilation

Co-articulation often leads to assimilation: one sound becomes more similar to a neighbouring sound. Assimilation can go in both directions, forward or backward, and it can be either the place of articulation or voice that is assimilated.

In progressive assimilation, a sound assimilates to the preceding sound. So the feature in which the sound becomes more similar is transmitted forward from one sound to the next. One movement of the speech organs is omitted: they remain in the same position when they should have moved to a different position for the new sound. That is why progressive assimilation is sometimes also called perseveratory assimilation.

In English, progressive assimilation is quite rare. However, it occurs in one important area: the inflectional suffixes (-ed) and plural/possessive (-s) assimilate to the preceding sound. They are realised as [d] and [z] when the preceding sound is also lenis/voiced in words such as ⟨moved⟩ [muːvd] or ⟨pens⟩ [pɛnz]. In words where the preceding sound is fortis/voiceless, however, the inflections are also realised fortis/voiceless as [t] and [s], as in ⟨talked⟩ [tɔːkt] or ⟨pets⟩ [pɛts]. In these cases, it is the feature of tension/voice that is assimilated and it is passed forward from one sound to the next.

Another case of progressive assimilation is syllabic [n̩] at the end of a word, in words such as ⟨open⟩ or ⟨happen⟩. Here an assimilation of the place of articulation takes place and [n] assimilates to the preceding sound and is consequently heard as either [m] when the preceding sound is also bilabial or [ŋ] when the preceding sound is velar. So instead of ['əʊ̯pn̩ ‖ 'oʊ̯pn̩] and ['hæpn̩], speakers will often pronounce ['əʊ̯pm̩ ‖ 'oʊ̯pm̩] and ['hæpm̩].

In regressive assimilation, the direction of the assimilation is the opposite: a sound assimilates to the one following it. While for progressive assimilation the speech organs remain in place too long, for regressive assimilation, their movement comes too early, so that a feature which should only occur later in the word can already be heard in an earlier sound. Because of this, regressive assimilation is sometimes also called anticipatory assimilation.

In English, regressive assimilation is frequent for syllable-final alveolar plosives and nasals [t, d, n]. The greeting ⟨Good morning⟩ is [gʊd 'mɔː(r)nɪŋ] when pronounced carefully. But in connected, everyday speech, [gʊb 'mɔː(r)nɪŋ] can be heard instead, where alveolar [d] has been replaced by bilabial [b] because of the following sound that is also bilabial. Similarly, ⟨ten coins⟩ may not in fact be pronounced as [tɛn 'kɔɪnz], but rather as [tɛŋ 'kɔɪnz] with a regressive assimilation of [n] to [ŋ].

Similar to [d] and [n], final [t] can become bilabial or velar. In many British accents, however, there is an increasing tendency to pronounce final [t] as a glottal stop. In this case, no regressive assimilation takes place.

/n/ → /m/	on paper	[ɒm 'peɪpə]	
	in between	[ɪm bi'twiːn]	
/n/ → /ŋ/	on call	[ɒŋ 'kɔːl]	
	incorrect	[ɪŋkə'rɛkt]	
/d/ → /b/	good boy	[gʊb 'bɔɪ]	
/d/ → /g/	good girl	[gʊg 'gɜːl]	
/t/ → /p/ or [ʔ]	football	['fʊpbɔːl]	['fʊʔbɔːl]
/t/ → /k/ or [ʔ]	that kid	[ðæk 'kɪd]	[ðæʔ 'kɪd]

Table 28: regressive assimilation

Assimilations can be very regular and even become lexicalised, i.e. included in the spelling of the word. While [tɛŋ 'kɔɪnz] becomes [tɛn 'kɔɪnz] again when it is spoken slowly, the word ⟨handkerchief⟩ is always pronounced ['hæŋkətʃɪf], never ['hænkətʃɪf], no matter how slowly someone speaks. A case where the assimilation has even been lexicalised is the prefix ⟨in-⟩: although it is spelt with ⟨n⟩ in most words such as ⟨informal⟩ or ⟨inappropriate⟩, the regressive assimilation of [n] can be seen in the spelling of words such as ⟨impossible⟩, ⟨illiterate⟩ or ⟨irregular⟩.

Coalescence

Coalescence [ˌkəʊəˈlɛsəns] is a special case of assimilation. The direction of the assimilation is neither progressive nor regressive, but two neighbouring sounds influence each other. The assimilation is reciprocal.

In English, coalescence frequently occurs when an alveolar obstruent (plosive or fricative) is followed by [j]. An alveolar plosive and [j] assimilate to an affricate. So the words (did you) (in careful pronunciation [dɪd juː]) are often pronounced as [dɪdʒuː] in casual speech. Similarly (can't you) [kɑːnt juː ‖ kænt juː] is assimilated to [kɑːntʃuː ‖ kæntʃuː]. In these examples, both the place and the manner of articulation change. The place of articulation is alveolar for [t] or [d] and palatal for [j]. For the outcome of the assimilation [tʃ] or [dʒ], the place of articulation is post-alveolar, which is in-between alveolar and palatal. The same could be said for the manner of articulation: while [t] and [d] as plosives are sounds of complete obstruction and [j] as an approximant has much more opening, the affricates [tʃ] and [dʒ] are somewhere in the middle ground.

When alveolar fricatives [s] or [z] are followed by [j], coalescence also occurs that results in post-alveolar fricatives. The phrase (this year), which in careful speech are pronounced as [ðɪs jɪə ‖ ðɪs jɪr], can be heard as [ðɪʃɪə ‖ ðɪʃɪr] in more rapid speech. Similarly, for (has your) the sound sequence [həz jɔː ‖ həz jʊr] assimilates to [həʒɔː ‖ həʒʊr]. Also in these cases, two sounds that are alveolar and palatal are merged into one sound that is post-alveolar.

/s/+/j/ → /ʃ/	this year	[ðɪs jɪə]	→ [ðɪʃɪə]
/z/+/j/ → /ʒ/	has your	[həz jɔː]	→ [həʒɔː]
/t/+/j/ → /tʃ/	can't you	[kɑːnt juː]	→ [kɑːntʃuː]
/d/+/j/ → /dʒ/	did you	[dɪd juː]	→ [dɪdʒuː]

Table 29: coalescence

Epenthesis

In cases of epenthesis [ɛˈpɛnθəsɪs], an additional phoneme is heard in the pronunciation of a word, which should not occur according to its spelling. In English, plosives are often inserted after nasals. These plosives are homorganic, meaning they have the same place of articulation as the preceding nasal.

Examples for epenthesis are words like (chance), (triumph) or (amongst). The pronunciation of these words is [tʃɑːns ‖ tʃæns], ['traɪ̯əmf] and [ə'mʌŋst]. However, many speakers will pronounce these words [tʃɑːnts ‖ tʃænts], ['traɪ̯əmpf] and [ə'mʌŋkst], which is equally correct. Here the plosives [t, p, k] have been inserted after the nasals [n, m, ŋ].

In terms of co-articulation, epenthesis can be seen as a case of anticipation: the speech organs already move into position for the following speech sound, although the articulation of the preceding speech sounds is not finished yet. It is the activity of the velum that leads to the insertion of the plosive. In the example of [tʃɑːns ‖ tʃæns], the velum is lowered for the nasal, so that the air can escape through the nose, while the tip of the tongue rests at the alveolar ridge. For the transition to [s], two things need to happen: firstly, the tip of the tongue needs to move away slightly from the alveolar ridge to create the narrowing for the fricative, and secondly, the velum needs to be raised to shut off the nasal passage. If the velum is raised earlier, however, before the oral obstacle at the alveolar ridge is released, the air stream accumulates at the alveolar ridge and will be heard as a plosive once the tongue finally moves away.

Elision and Compression

In rapid speech, when the articulatory movements of the speech organs have to become quicker, sounds not only become shorter, but they can disappear entirely. Elision [i'lɪʒn̩] is the full deletion of a phoneme from the pronunciation of a word.

In English, vowels in unaccented syllables are reduced to schwa [ə]. So in the word (camera) only the first syllable contains a full vowel, while vowel quality is obscured and reduced to schwa in the last two syllables: ['kæmərə]. Ultimately, schwa can be deleted entirely: ['kæmrə]. Similarly, the word (police) [pə'liːs] is pronounced by many speakers with one syllable only: [pliːs]. In these examples, elision as the deletion of a speech sound occurs together with compression, which is the loss of a syllable. While ['kæmərə] has three syllables, ['kæmrə] only has two.

Also consonants, especially [t] or [d], can be deleted, namely when they occur in the middle of a consonant cluster. In the phrase (last night) [lɑːst 'naɪt ‖ læst 'naɪt], three consonants follow consecutively [stn]. In connected speech, this cluster is simplified by dropping the [t], so that speakers pronounce [lɑːs 'naɪt ‖ læs 'naɪt] instead. Another example is ⟨next week⟩ where there is even a cluster of four consonants: [nɛkst 'wiːk]. Here again, many speakers will delete the [t], simplifying the consonant cluster to [nɛks 'wiːk].

While [t] deletion was a case of elision without compression, compression can also occur without elision. The word ⟨obedient⟩, for instance, can be pronounced [ə 'biː di ənt] with four syllables. It is equally possible, however, that it becomes [ə 'biː djənt] with one syllable less. For ⟨threatening⟩, the pronunciations ['θrɛt n̩ ɪŋ] or ['θrɛt n̩ɪŋ] are both possible. In the latter, the syllabic [n̩] loses its status as a syllable and becomes part of the last syllable. Three syllables are compressed into two.

Linking

Words are linked across word boundaries in English. For speakers with German as their mother tongue, this is especially difficult when the next word starts with a vowel as Germans insert a glottal stop whenever a syllable starts with a vowel making it sound staccato to an English ear.

In English, quite the contrary is the case. When the following word starts with a vowel, the last consonant of the preceding word is used as a bridge that links to the next word. That is why it may sound as if this consonant belongs to the following word. To a foreign language learner, the phrase ⟨at all⟩ therefore sounds more like [ə tɔːl] rather than [ət ɔːl].

eine alte Eiche	vs.	*an old oak*
[ʔaɛ̯nə ǀ ʔaltə ǀ ʔaɛ̯çə]		[ən‿əʊ̯ld‿əʊ̯k]

Received Pronunciation is a non-rhotic accent. ⟨r⟩ after a vowel is therefore not pronounced. Instead, a centring diphthong can be heard as in ⟨fear⟩ [fɪə̯] or ⟨scare⟩ [skɛə̯] or nothing at all as in ⟨far⟩ [fɑː] or ⟨more⟩ [mɔː]. In connected speech, however, when a word ending with postvocalic ⟨r⟩ is followed by a word that starts with a vowel, the [r] is pronounced to facilitate linking. We then speak of a linking [r].

word in isolation		linking (r)	
store	[stɔ:]	store away	[stɔ:r əweɪ̯]
director	[daɪ̯rɛktə]	director of	[daɪ̯rɛktər əv]
more	[mɔ:]	more of	[mɔ:r əv]
here	[hɪə̯]	here is	[hɪə̯r ɪz]
far	[fɑ:]	far away	[fɑ:r əweɪ̯]

Table 30: linking [r]

The phenomenon of linking one word to another word starting with a vowel goes even further. Words such as (more), (shore), (door), (poor) or (store) are typical candidates for linking [r]. However, there are many words that have the same sound structure but have in fact no (r) in their spelling: (draw), (saw) or (law). Because these words sound the same as the ones where linking [r] can occur, speakers insert an intrusive [r] in connected speech, even though there is none in the spelling.

word in isolation		intrusive (r)	
draw	[drɔ:]	draw a circle	[drɔ:r ə sɜ:kl̩]
saw	[sɔ:]	saw an accident	[sɔ:r ən æksɪdənt]
idea	[aɪ̯dɪə̯]	idea of his	[aɪ̯dɪə̯r əv hɪz]
law	[lɔ:]	law and order	[lɔ:r ənd ɔ:də]

Table 31: intrusive [r]

As General American is a rhotic accent and (r) is always pronounced when it occurs in the spelling, neither linking nor intrusive [r] occur in this variety.

Exercises

8.1

The author's of the following books have telling names. Read their names with linking and find an English word or phrase that sounds alike.

1) *At the South* Pole by Ann Tarctic
2) *Swimming the Channel* by Frances Near
3) *The Bullfighter* by Matt Adore
4) *The Unknown Author* by Ann Onymous
5) *The Long Hot Summer* by I. Scream
6) *A Cliff-top Tragedy* by Eileen Dover
7) *The Cause of Colds* by Mike Robe
8) *The Escaping Sheep* by Gay Topen
9) *The Return of the Prodigal* Son by Gladys Back
10) *Sent to Jail* by Robin Banks
11) *The Proper Use of Sunscreens* by Justin Casey Burns
12) *Crossing the Desert* by I. Rhoda Camel
13) *Mountain Climbing* by Hugo First
14) *Set Fire to the Taxman* by Bernadette Collector
15) *Watching African Animals* by Anne T. Lope

8.2

Transcribe the following phrases. Which phonological processes could occur in connected speech?

in case	*drawing*	*gardening*	*facts*	*history*
just then	*monster*	*four eggs*	*input*	*hamster*
I need you	*didn't dare*	*on purpose*	*as you know*	*bacon*

8.3

Transcribe the following passage from *The Wonderful Wizard of Oz* by L. Frank Baum.

After a few hours the road began to be rough, and the walking grew so difficult that the Scarecrow often stumbled over the yellow bricks, which were here very uneven. Sometimes, indeed, they were broken or missing altogether, leaving holes that Toto jumped across and Dorothy walked around. As for the Scarecrow, having no brains, he walked straight ahead, and so stepped into the holes and fell at full length on the hard bricks. It never hurt him, however, and Dorothy would pick him up and set him upon his feet again, while he joined her in laughing merrily at his own mishap.

 Listen to a recording of the transcription text online at: www.phonetiker.net/transcript/

8.4

Read the following IPA transcription from *A Study in Scarlet* by Sir Arthur Conan Doyle and write the text orthographically.

[ðɪs wəz ə ˈlɒfti ˈtʃeɪmbə | laɪnd ənd ˈlɪtəd wɪð kaʊ̯ntləs ˈbɒtl̩z ‖ brɔːd ləʊ̯ ˈteɪ̯bl̩z wə skætəd əˈbaʊ̯t | wɪtʃ brɪsl̩d wɪð riˈtɔːts ˈtɛstjuːbz ənd lɪtl̩ ˈbʌnsn̩ læmps | wɪð ðɛə̯ bluː flɪkərɪŋ ˈfleɪ̯mz ‖ ðɛə̯ wəz əʊ̯nli wʌn ˈstjuːdn̩t ɪn ðə ˈruːm | hu wəz bɛndɪŋ əʊ̯vər ə dɪstənt ˈteɪ̯bl̩ | əbˈzɔːbd ɪn hɪz ˈwɜːk ‖ ət ðə saʊ̯nd əv aʊ̯ə ˈstɛps | hi glɑːnst ˈraʊ̯nd | ənd spræŋ tə hɪz ˈfiːt wɪð ə kraɪ̯ əv ˈplɛʒə]

[ðɪs wəz ə ˈlɔːfti ˈtʃeɪmbɚ | laɪnd ənd ˈlɪtɚd wɪθ kaʊ̯ntləs ˈbɑːtl̩z ‖ brɔːd loʊ̯ ˈteɪ̯bl̩z wɚ skætɚd əˈbaʊ̯t | wɪtʃ brɪsl̩d wɪθ riˈtɔːrts ˈtɛstuːbz ənd lɪtl̩ ˈbʌnsn̩ læmps | wɪθ ðɛr bluː flɪkɚɪŋ ˈfleɪ̯mz ‖ ðɛr wəz oʊ̯nli wʌn ˈstuːdn̩t ɪn ðə ˈruːm | hu wəz bɛndɪŋ oʊ̯vɚ ə dɪstənt ˈteɪ̯bl̩ | əbˈzɔːrbd ɪn hɪz ˈwɝːk ‖ ət ðə saʊ̯nd əv aʊ̯ɚ ˈstɛps | hi glænst ˈraʊ̯nd | ənd spræŋ tə hɪz ˈfiːt wɪθ ə kraɪ̯ əv ˈplɛʒɚ]

 Listen to a recording of the transcription text online at: www.phonetiker.net/transcript/

9 Syllables
['sɪləb̩z]

The syllable is an intermediate unit between the phonemes of a word and the word as a whole. A word consists of one or more syllables. While even children at primary school have no problem with segmenting a word into its syllables, the phonetic and phonological basis of this demands some consideration.

Syllable Structure

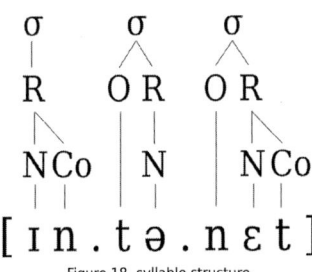

Figure 18. syllable structure

The word (internet) consists of three syllables: ['ɪn.tə.nɛt ‖ 'ɪn.tɚ.nɛt]. The centre of a syllable is called nucleus ['njuːkliəs ‖ 'nuːkliəs]. The nucleus is most often a vowel, but it can also be a syllabic nasal or lateral. Consonants that follow the nucleus are called the coda. Nucleus and coda together form the rhyme, which is easy to remember, as two words rhyme that have the same rhyme. Any consonants before the nucleus are called onset. Onset together with rhyme form the syllable, which is given the Greek letter sigma (σ).

Onsets and codas are optional in English, as can be seen in the example. A maximum of three consonants can stand in the onset. The coda can contain a maximum of four consonants. Therefore, the smallest syllable structure is V, consisting of only one vowel, and the maximum structure is CCCVCCCC. The most common syllable is CV in English.

coda

onset	0 ...V	1 ...VC	2 ...VCC	3 ...VCCC	4 ...VCCCC
0 V...	*eye* [aɪ̯]	*eat* [iːt]	*end* [ɛnd]	*ants* [ænts]	*pre-empts* [ɛmpts]
1 CV...	*day* [deɪ̯]	*book* [bʊk]	*health* [hɛlθ]	*helped* [hɛlpt]	*texts* [tɛksts]
2 CCV...	*stay* [steɪ̯]	*speak* [spiːk]	*trend* [trɛnd]	*prints* [prɪnts]	*glimpsed* [glɪmpst]
3 CCCV...	*spray* [spreɪ̯]	*screen* [skriːn]	*sprint* [sprɪnt]	*strands* [strændz]	*strengths* [strɛŋkθs]

Table 32: examples for onset and coda clusters in English

 *caring power of sound*

Sonority Sequencing Generalisation

The question of how many syllables a word consists of is related to the sonority of the sounds the word contains. Sonority can be translated as the 'carrying power' of a sound. A sound with higher sonority will be heard as louder and will carry farther than a sound with lower sonority. For instance, [ɑ:] as a low vowel has a very high degree of sonority, as the vocal folds vibrate and the mouth is fully open, so that the sound can leave the oral cavity with its full intensity. In comparison, [f] is much less sonorant with the only sound being friction between lips and teeth.

A scale can be established that compares the different speech sounds in their degree of sonority. This scale is called the Sonority Sequencing Generalisation. At the top are low vowels with the highest degree of sonority, at the bottom voiceless plosives with the lowest degree.

low vowels	
high vowels	
lateral	
nasals	
approximants	
fricatives	
affricates	
plosives	

always nucleus

___

can become nucleus
(syllabic consonants [n̩], [l̩])

never nucleus
only onset or coda

Figure 19: sonority sequencing generalisation

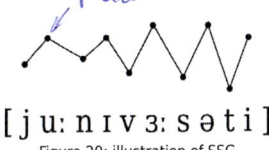

peaks are number of syllables

[j u: n ɪ v ɜ: s ə t i]

Figure 20: illustration of SSG

Sounds with high sonority form the centre of a syllable, the nucleus. From the centre of the syllable towards its periphery, sonority decreases gradually. Considering the syllable as a whole, sonority is low in the onset, increases towards the nucleus and decreases again in the coda.

A word has as many syllables as it has nuclei [ˈnjuːkliaɪ ‖ ˈnuːkliaɪ] or peaks of sonority. This becomes apparent when comparing the English words ⟨sand⟩ and ⟨sadden⟩ or the German examples ⟨Halm⟩ and ⟨Hammel⟩. The words [sænd] and [halm] both consist of one syllable. There is an increase in sonority from the onset [s] or [h] to the nucleus [æ] or [a]. From there, the sonority decreases gradually: in ⟨sand⟩, [n] has lower sonority than [æ] and [d] has lower sonority than [n]. In ⟨Halm⟩, [l] has lower sonority than [a] and [m] is less sonorant than [l].

For the words ⟨sadden⟩ and ⟨Hammel⟩, the picture is quite different. They consist of the same phonemes, but the order of the last two sounds is reversed: [ˈsædn] and [ˈhaml]. In terms of sonority, this means that the sonority drops after the nucleus, but increases again with the next consonant: [n] and [l] show a higher degree of sonority than [d] and [m] respectively. Because of that, the last sound forms another nucleus and the word is heard as consisting of two syllables: [ˈsæ.dn̩], [ˈha.ml̩]. The stroke under the [n] and [l] indicates that these sounds form a nucleus, they are syllabic.

Maximum Onset Principle

[handwritten: as much consonants into onset rather than in coda]

Once the nuclei within a word have been identified with help of the Sonority Sequencing Generalisation, the question remains how the consonants in-between two nuclei should be treated: should they be attributed to the preceding syllable or to the following one? The word ⟨internet⟩, for example, quite clearly consists of three syllables with the three nuclei [ɪ], [ə] and [ɛ]. As for the distribution of consonants, there are several possible syllabifications.

- [ˈɪ.ntə.nɛt]
- [ˈɪ.ntən.ɛt]
- [ˈɪn.tə.nɛt]
- [ˈɪn.tən.ɛt]
- [ˈɪnt.ə.nɛt]
- [ˈɪnt.ən.ɛt]

[handwritten: [ɪn.tə.nɛt]]

While in this example, it is quite clear that only [ˈɪn.tə.nɛt] can possibly be the correct syllabification, there are cases which are not as clear-cut. For the word ⟨diplomat⟩, for instance, most native speakers will be hesitant whether [ˈdɪp.lə.mæt] or [ˈdɪ.plə.mæt] is correct. Another example is ⟨master⟩, for which both, [ˈmɑːs.tə ‖ ˈmæs.tɚ] and [ˈmɑː.stə ‖ ˈmæ.stɚ], seem to be equally acceptable.

Whether a phoneme is attributed to the preceding or the following syllable has consequences for its position within that syllable. If a consonant is attributed to the preceding syllable, it forms the coda of that syllable. Attributed to the following syllable, it will be part of its onset.

Languages show different preferences for onsets and codas. In English, only the nucleus is an obligatory element. Both onsets and codas are optional. There are syllables such as ⟨I⟩ [aɪ̯] that only consist of a nucleus. Across the languages of the world, however, there seems to be a clear preference for syllable onsets rather than codas. Some languages, such as German, demand an onset: no syllable can start with a nucleus. The word ⟨Ei⟩, for instance, is realised as [ʔaɪ̯] with a glottal stop as the onset. Other languages have severe restrictions on codas: either only selected single consonants are allowed, as in Japanese, or codas are forbidden entirely, as in Hawaiian, where all syllables must end with the nucleus. Because of this distribution, if possible, sounds should always be attributed to an onset rather than to a coda. This principle is called the Maximum Onset Principle.

Phonotactic Constraints

There are restrictions, however, how many and which consonants can occur in syllable onsets and codas. Which combinations of sounds may or may not occur in a language are called phonotactic constraints. Phonotactic constraints for syllable onsets in English state, for instance, that while many syllables start with [pl] as in ⟨please⟩ or with [gl] as in ⟨glass⟩, the combination [dl] is not possible. These restrictions are language-specific. In English, [str] is a possible onset in words like ⟨street⟩. [ftr], however, is not found in English, while Greek allows this combination.

Even if onset or coda only contain one consonant phoneme, restrictions apply. [ŋ] and [ʒ] never occur in onsets, but only in codas. [h] as well as the approximants [j] and [w], on the other hand, can occur in onsets, but not in codas.

Syllable onsets in English cannot contain more than three consonants. If the onset contains two consonants, the second consonant is always one of the approximants [l, r, j, w]. Only if the first consonant is [s] or [ʃ], other consonants can also occur in second position, such as [t] in ⟨stick⟩, [p] in ⟨sport⟩ or [k] in ⟨skin⟩. If the onset contains three consonants, the first consonant can only be [s], the second one will be a fortis plosive [p, t, k] and the third an approximant [l, r, j, w].

pl	bl	tl	dl	kl	gl	ml	nl	fl	vl		sl	ʃl		
pr	br	tr	dr	kr	gr			fr	vr	θr		ʃr		
pj	bj	tj	dj	kj	gj	mj	nj	fj	vj	θj	sj		hj	lj
pw	bw	tw	dw	kw	gw	mw	nw			θw	sw	ʃw		
											sp, st, sk, sm, sn, sf, sv, ʃp, ʃt, ʃm, ʃn			

(handwritten additions: tl, dl, ml, nl in row 1; pw, bw, nw in row 4)

Table 33: two-consonant clusters in English

spl		skl
spr	str	skr
spj	stj	skj
		skw

Table 34: three-consonant clusters in English

(handwritten notes)

two - consonant cluster:

consonant +

Approximat [l, r/w/n, j]

three - consonant cluster

[s] + fortis plosive +

approximant [l, r, j, w]

Another constraint is imposed by the checked nature of short vowels in English. If a syllable is stressed and contains a short vowel, this syllable should not end with the vowel, but another consonant must follow. Therefore, the syllabification of ⟨system⟩ is ['sɪs.təm] rather than ['sɪ.stəm], even though phonotactic constraints would allow [st] as an onset cluster.

Exercises

9.1

Syllabify the following words and draw a syllable tree:

    a) *extract*
    b) *juncture*
    c) *magnitude*
    d) *district*

9.2

Decide whether the following non-sense words are admissible in English.

[freɪ̯h]	[ʃvɛk]	[ʒɪlf]
[sprʊŋk]	[knəʊ̯]	[skwɒltʃ]

9.3

The Japanese language borrowed the following words from English or
German. Can you explain the difference in pronunciation?
([ɯ] is unrounded [u], [tɕ dʑ] are similar to [tʃ dʒ])

Christmas	クリスマス	[kɯ.ri.sɯ.ma.sɯ]
sandwich	サンドイッチ	[san.dɔ.i. tɕi]
milk	ミルク	[mi.rɯ.kɯ]
table	テーブル	[teː.bɯ.rɯ]
McDonald's	マクドナルド	[ma.kɯ.dɔ.na.rɯ.tɔ]
Arbeit	アルバイト	[a.rɯ.ba.i.tɔ]
Düsseldorf	デュッセルドルフ	[dʑɯ.sse.rɯ.dɔ.rɯ.fɯ]

9.4

Transcribe the following passage from *Dracula* by Bram Stoker.

Then with swiftness, but with absolute method, Van Helsing performed the
operation. As the transfusion went on, something like life seemed to come
back to poor Lucy's cheeks, and through Arthur's growing pallor the joy of
his face seemed absolutely to shine. After a bit I began to grow anxious, for
the loss of blood was telling on Arthur, strong man as he was. It gave me an
idea of what a terrible strain Lucy's system must have undergone that what
weakened Arthur only partially restored her.

Listen to a recording of the transcription text online at:
www.phonetiker.net/transcript/

9.5

Read the following IPA transcription from *The Island of Doctor Moreau* by H. G. Wells and write the text orthographically.

 [səʊ̯ aɪ̯ leɪ̯ 'stɪl ðɛə̯ | ʌntɪl aɪ̯ bɪgæn tə 'θɪŋk əv fu:d ənd 'drɪŋk | ənd ət 'ðæt θɔːt | ðə riːəl 'həʊ̯pləsnəs əv maɪ̯ pə'zɪʃn̩ | keɪ̯m 'həʊ̯m tə mi: ‖ aɪ̯ nju: nəʊ̯ 'weɪ̯ əv gɛtɪŋ ɛniθɪŋ tu 'iːt ‖ aɪ̯ wəz tu: 'ɪgnərənt əv bɒtəni | tə dɪskʌvər ɛni ri'zɔːt əv ruːt ɔ: 'fruːt | ðət maɪ̯t laɪ̯ ə'baʊ̯t mi: | aɪ̯ həd nəʊ̯ 'miːnz əv træpɪŋ ðə fju: 'ræbɪts əpɒn ði aɪ̯lənd ‖ ɪt gruː 'blæŋkə | ðə mɔːr aɪ̯ tɜːnd ðə prɒspɛkt 'əʊ̯və ‖ ət 'lɑːst | ɪn ðə dɛspə'reɪ̯ʃn̩ əv maɪ̯ pə'zɪʃn̩ | maɪ̯ 'maɪ̯nd tɜːnd tə ði 'ænɪml̩ mɛn aɪ̯ həd ɪnkaʊ̯ntəd ‖ aɪ̯ traɪ̯d tə faɪ̯nd səm 'həʊ̯p | ɪn wɒt aɪ̯ rɪ'mɛmbəd əv ðəm]

 [soʊ̯ aɪ̯ leɪ̯ 'stɪl ðɛr | ʌntɪl aɪ̯ bɪgæn tə 'θɪŋk əv fu:d ənd 'drɪŋk | ənd ət 'ðæt θɔːt | ðə riːəl 'hoʊ̯pləsnəs əv maɪ̯ pə'zɪʃn̩ | keɪ̯m 'hoʊ̯m tə mi: ‖ aɪ̯ nu: noʊ̯ 'weɪ̯ əv gɛtɪŋ ɛniθɪŋ tu 'iːt ‖ aɪ̯ wəz tu: 'ɪgnərənt əv bɑːtəni | tə dɪskʌvɚ ɛni ri'zɔːrt əv ruːt ɔːr 'fruːt | ðət maɪ̯t laɪ̯ ə'baʊ̯t mi: | aɪ̯ həd noʊ̯ 'miːnz əv træpɪŋ ðə fju: 'ræbɪts əpɑːn ði aɪ̯lənd ‖ ɪt gruː 'blæŋkɚ | ðə mɔːr aɪ̯ tɝːnd ðə prɑːspɛkt 'oʊ̯vɚ ‖ ət 'læst | ɪn ðə dɛspə'reɪ̯ʃn̩ əv maɪ̯ pə'zɪʃn̩ | maɪ̯ 'maɪ̯nd tɝːnd tə ði 'ænɪml̩ mɛn aɪ̯ həd ɪnkaʊ̯ntɚd ‖ aɪ̯ traɪ̯d tə faɪ̯nd səm 'hoʊ̯p | ɪn wʌt aɪ̯ rɪ'mɛmbɚd əv ðəm]

Listen to a recording of the transcription text online at: www.phonetiker.net/transcript/

10 Word Stress
['wɜːd strɛs]

Word Stress in English

Word stress means, that in any word that has two or more syllables, one syllable stands out from the others, i.e. it is stressed. In the word (morning), the first syllable is stressed while the word (afternoon) has stress on the last syllable. In IPA, stress is marked with ['] before the stressed syllable: ['mɔːnɪŋ ‖ 'mɔːrnɪŋ] and [ɑːftə'nuːn ‖ æftɚ'nuːn].

A syllable is perceived as stressed when it is either louder or higher in pitch than the surrounding syllables. To a lesser degree, also vowel quality and length may play a role.

In English, word stress is both variable and fixed. It is variable because it is not always the same syllable that is stressed. In numerous languages, word stress is always on the same syllable: in French, it is always the last syllable that is stressed, in Czech, it is always the first syllable, in Polish, the last-but-one syllable. In English, on the other hand, word stress can, in principle, occur on any syllable of a word. Despite this seeming variability, the position of the stressed syllable for individual English words is in fact fixed and an integral part of the pronunciation of a word.

English is a Germanic language and its stress pattern follows that of many Germanic languages: word stress is on the first syllable of the stem.

manage	['mænɪʤ]
manager	['mænɪʤə]
management	['mænɪʤmənt]
mismanage	[mɪs'mænɪʤ]
helpful	['hɛlpfʊl]
helping	['hɛlpɪŋ]
unhelpful	[ʌn'hɛlpfʊl]

Table 35: Germanic stress pattern

However, there are many exceptions to the Germanic stress pattern. Because of the Norman conquest, a large portion of the English vocabulary is in fact not Germanic, but of French or Latin origin. In such words, it is often not the first syllable of the stem that receives word stress but a different one.

Which syllable is stressed in a word has far-reaching consequences. Unstressed syllables become reduced, in English more radically than in many other languages. If we compare the words ⟨a present⟩ ['prɛznt̩] and ⟨to present⟩ [prɪ'zɛnt]: the noun is stressed on the first syllable, the verb on the last. In both cases, there is a full vowel in the stressed syllable. In the unstressed syllable of ⟨to present⟩, the vowel becomes reduced to [ɪ], in ⟨a present⟩ it is completely absent, so that only syllabic [n̩] is left. Depending on which syllable is accentuated, the entire pronunciation of a word changes. Therefore, word stress must be learnt together with the word as stressing the wrong syllable will often render a word incomprehensible.

Zero-Derivation

Derivation is the process of creating a new word by adding a suffix or prefix. Also, in order to change the word class of a word, e.g. from noun to verb, derivative suffixes are added. ⟨-ous⟩, for instance, turns a noun into an adjective: ⟨courage⟩ becomes ⟨courageous⟩. In German, ⟨-en⟩ is a verbal suffix. So, in order to use ⟨Mail⟩ as a verb, ⟨-en⟩ needs to be added ⟨mailen⟩.

Zero-derivation is a special kind of derivation quite frequent in English where the word class changes without a suffix being added. ⟨butter⟩, for instance, is a noun but it can easily be used as a verb ⟨to butter⟩. Words created through zero-derivation are identical in spelling. The pronunciation, however, often differs.

Where a word can be used both as a noun and a verb, the noun is stressed on the first syllable while the verb has stress on a later, mostly the last syllable. When a verb can equally be used as an adjective, it is again the verb that has late stress while the adjective is stressed on the first syllable.

	noun	verb	adjective
import	['ɪm pɔːt]	[ɪm 'pɔːt]	
permit	['pɜː mɪt]	[pə 'mɪt]	
protest	['prəʊ tɛst]	[prə 'tɛst]	
record	['rɛk ɔːd]	[ri 'kɔːd]	
survey	['sɜː veɪ]	[sə 'veɪ]	
transport	['træns pɔːt]	[træns 'pɔːt]	
present	['prɛz n̩t]	[prɪ 'zɛnt]	
object	['ɒb dʒɛkt]	[əb 'dʒɛkt]	
update	['ʌp deɪt]	[ʌp 'deɪt]	
produce	['prɒd juːs]	[prə 'djuːs]	
rebel	['rɛb l̩]	[rɪ 'bɛl]	
refuse	['rɛf juːs]	[ri 'fjuːz]	
overlap	['əʊ və læp]	[əʊ və 'læp]	
overflow	['əʊ və fləʊ]	[əʊ və 'fləʊ]	
outlay	['aʊt leɪ]	[aʊt 'leɪ]	
uplift	['ʌp lɪft]	[ʌp 'lɪft]	
attribute	['æt rɪ bjuːt]	[ə 'trɪ bjuːt]	
abstract	['æb strækt]	[æb 'strækt]	['æb strækt]
subject	['sʌb dʒɛkt]	[səb 'dʒɛkt]	['sʌb dʒɛkt]
content	['kɒn tɛnt]	[kən 'tɛnt]	[kən 'tɛnt]
absent		[æb 'sɛnt]	['æb sənt]
frequent		[frɪ 'kwɛnt]	['friː kwənt]
perfect		[pə 'fɛkt]	['pɜː fɪkt]

Table 36: zero-derivation and stress shift

For zero-derivatives, as for all words in general, word stress has an impact on vowel quality. While the stressed syllable contains a full vowel, in an unstressed syllable, vowel quality becomes reduced and obscured to [ə] or [ɪ].

Listen to recordings of zero-derivatives online at:
www.phonetiker.net/transcript/

Compounds

Two independent words can be put together to form a new word in its own right, a compound. In German, compounds are joined and written as one word. In English, this is not necessarily the case. As the primary medium of language is its spoken form, the question should not be so much whether a compound is written together or not, but rather whether one can hear that it is a compound.

Nominal compounds (compounds functioning as nouns) have initial stress in English, i.e. the first of the two words is stressed. However, if the two words do not form a compound, but simply happen to stand next to each other within a sentence, they are both stressed. We then speak of level stress. For instance, a ⟨darkroom⟩ is a special room photographers use to develop their prints. As darkroom is a nominal compound, it is stressed on the first word only, on ⟨dark⟩. If, on the other hand, speakers talk about a room that is dark, just as they could talk about a bright room, both words are equally stressed.

	nominal compound	free phrase
black( )board	"chalkboard" ['blæk bɔːd]	"board that is black" ['blæk 'bɔːd]
English teacher	"who teaches English" ['ɪŋglɪʃ tiːtʃə]	"comes from England" ['ɪŋglɪʃ 'tiːtʃə]
dark( )room	"photo laboratory" ['dɑːk ruːm]	"room with no light" ['dɑːk 'ruːm]
blue( )print	"type of copy" ['bluː prɪnt]	"print that is blue" ['bluː 'prɪnt]
white house / White House	"seat of US President" ['waɪt haʊs]	"house that is white" ['waɪt 'haʊs]
	initial stress	**level stress**

Table 37: stress in nominal compounds vs. free phrases

Generally, nominal compounds receive initial stress. There are, however, two exceptions that can be summarized as the Manufacturer's Rule and the Location Rule.

The Manufacturer's Rule states that a nominal compound does not receive initial but level stress when it is made of the material it specifies.

Therefore, in compounds like ⟨apple pie⟩, ⟨paper bag⟩ or ⟨wooden doll⟩ both words are stressed since they fall under the Manufacturer's Rule: ['æpl̩ 'paɪ], ['peɪpə 'bæg ‖ 'peɪpɚ 'bæg] and ['wʊdn̩ 'dɒl ‖ 'wʊdn̩ 'dɑːl]. Other compounds such as ⟨apple tree⟩, ⟨paper clip⟩ or ⟨wood cutter⟩ are stressed on the first component only because they do not specify the material they are made of. The pronunciation is hence ['æpl̩ triː], ['peɪpə klɪp ‖ 'peɪpɚ klɪp] and ['wʊd kʌtə ‖ 'wʊd kʌtɚ].

The Location Rule says that compounds which contain a location receive level stress. Therefore, place names such as ⟨King's Cross⟩, ⟨Waterloo Station⟩, ⟨Oxford Circus⟩ or ⟨Silicon Valley⟩ are stressed on both components of the compound: ['kɪŋz 'krɒs ‖ 'kɪŋz 'krɔːs], [wɔːtə'luː 'steɪʃn̩ ‖ wɔːtɚ'luː 'steɪʃn̩], ['ɒksfəd 'sɜːkəs ‖ 'ɑːksfɚd 'sɜ˞ːkəs] and ['sɪlɪkən 'væli]. Only place names that contain ⟨Street⟩ do not fall under the Location rule and are pronounced with initial stress.

Adjective compounds which contain an ⟨-ed⟩-participle are pronounced with level stress when they stand in predicative position after the verb. Thus, where German has initial stress in ⟨altmodisch⟩ ['ʔaltmoːdɪʃ], the English adjective has level stress ⟨old-fashioned⟩ ['əʊld 'fæʃn̩d]. However, when such adjectives are used attributively before a noun, the stress pattern changes to initial stress.

predicative level stress	He is quite absent-minded.	['æbsənt 'maɪndɪd]
	Managers are overpaid.	['əʊvə 'peɪd]
	That's quite short-sighted.	['ʃɔːt 'saɪtɪd]
	The marriage was short-lived.	['ʃɔːt 'lɪvd]
	This girl is blue-eyed.	['bluː 'aɪd]
attributive initial stress	an absent-minded professor	['æbsənt maɪndɪd]
	the overpaid manager	['əʊvə peɪd]
	a short-sighted person	['ʃɔːt saɪtɪd]
	a short-lived market	['ʃɔːt lɪvd]
	such a blue-eyed boy	['bluː aɪd]

Table 38: stress in adjective-participle compounds

 Listen to recordings of compounds online at:
www.phonetiker.net/transcript/

Stress-Shifting Suffixes

The majority of prefixes and suffixes are stress-neutral and do not lead to a change in stress pattern: the stress remains on the same syllable as in the word without the affix. Among them are the prefixes (un-) and (mis-) that are frequently stressed in German, but not in English.

to address	[əˈdrɛs]
addressable	[əˈdrɛsəbl̩]
unaddressable	[ʌnəˈdrɛsəbl̩] not [ˈʌnədrɛsəbl̩]

However, many suffixes of foreign origin lead to a change in stress pattern. A different syllable is stressed than in the word without the suffix.

address	[əˈdrɛs]
addressee	[ædrɛˈsiː] not [əˈdrɛsiː]

Suffixes that lead to a change in the stress pattern of a word are called stress-shifting suffixes. Three different types of stress-shifting suffixes can be distinguished. Words containing stress-carrying suffixes are stressed on the ultimate (or last) syllable, as the suffix is stressed itself. The other two possibilities are that the word is stressed on the penultimate (last-but-one) or antepenultimate (last-but-two) syllable. Suffixes that cause such a pronunciation change are called stress-repelling suffixes, since they are not stressed themselves, but still trigger a change in word stress.

The first group of stress-shifting suffixes are stress-carrying suffixes. In words that end with one of these suffixes, it is the suffix itself that receives stress. So, for instance, the country (Japan) is stressed on the second syllable. The adjective (Japanese), however, is stressed on the last syllable because (-ese) is a stress-carrying suffix.

suffix	example	without suffix	with stress shift
-ade	*cannonade*	['kæn ən]	→ [kæ nə 'neɪd]
	lemonade	['lɛm ən]	→ [lɛ mə 'neɪd]
-ee	*addressee*	[ə 'drɛs]	→ [ə drɛ 'siː]
	employee	[ɪm 'plɔɪ]	→ [ɪm plɔɪ 'iː]
-eer	*engineer*	['ɛn ʤɪn]	→ [ɛn ʤɪ 'nɪə]
	profiteer	['prɒf ɪt]	→ [prɒ fɪ 'tɪə]
-ese	*Chinese*	['ʧaɪ nə]	→ [ʧaɪ 'niːz]
	Japanese	[ʤə 'pæn]	→ [ʤæ pə 'niːz]
-esque	*picturesque*	['pɪk ʧə]	→ [pɪk ʧə 'rɛsk]
	romanesque	['rəʊ mən]	→ [rəʊ mə 'nɛsk]
-ette	*cigarette*	[sɪ 'gɑː]	→ [sɪ gə 'rɛt]
	kitchenette	['kɪʧ n̩]	→ [kɪ ʧə 'nɛt]
-ier	*grenadier*	[grə 'neɪd]	→ [grɛ nə 'dɪə]
	cashier	['kæʃ]	→ [kæ 'ʃɪə]
-ique	*technique*	['tɛk nɪ kəl]	→ [tɛk 'niːk]
	critique	['krɪt ɪ kəl]	→ [krɪ 'tiːk]
-oon	*balloon*	['bɔːl]	→ [bə 'luːn]
	cartoon	['kɑː tən]	→ [kɑː 'tuːn]

Table 39: stress-carrying suffixes

Other suffixes are stress-repelling. Similar to stress-carrying suffixes, they are not stress-neutral, but lead to a shift in the stress pattern of the word. Unlike stress-carrying suffixes, however, they are not stressed themselves, but push the stress to the preceding syllable: the last-but-one syllable, referred to as the penultimate [pəˈnʌltɪmət] syllable.

suffix	example	without suffix	with stress shift
-tion	*concentration*	[ˈkɒn sn̩ treɪt]	→ [kɒn sn̩ ˈtreɪ ʃn̩]
	permission	[ˈpɜː mɪt]	→ [pə ˈmɪʃ n̩]
-eous	*courageous*	[ˈkʌr ɪʤ]	→ [kə ˈreɪ ʤəs]
	outrageous	[ˈaʊt reɪʤ]	→ [aʊt ˈreɪ ʤəs]
-ial	*industrial*	[ˈɪn də stri]	→ [ɪn ˈdʌs trɪəl]
	editorial	[ˈɛd ɪ tə]	→ [ɛ dɪ ˈtɔː rɪəl]
-ian	*musician*	[ˈmju: zɪk]	→ [mju: ˈzɪʃ n̩]
	comedian	[ˈkɒm ə di]	→ [kə ˈmi: djən]
-ic	*academic*	[ə ˈkæd ə mi]	→ [æ kə ˈdɛm ɪk]
	automatic	[ˈɔː tə meɪt]	→ [ɔː tə ˈmæt ɪk]
-ious	*suspicious*	[ˈsʌs pɛkt]	→ [sə ˈspɪʃ əs]
	fictitious	[ˈfɪk ʃn̩]	→ [fɪk ˈtɪʃ əs]
-itis	*appendicitis*	[ə ˈpɛn dɪks]	→ [ə pɛn də ˈsaɪ tɪs]
	tonsillitis	[ˈtɒn sɪlz]	→ [tɒn sə ˈlaɪ tɪs]
-ental	*accidental*	[ˈæk sɪ dənt]	→ [æk sɪ ˈdɛn təl]
	instrumental	[ˈɪn strə mənt]	→ [ɪn strə ˈmɛn tl̩]
-ual	*habitual*	[ˈhæb ɪt]	→ [hə ˈbɪt ʊəl]
	conceptual	[ˈkɒn sɛpt]	→ [kən ˈsɛp tʊəl]
-uous	*continuous*	[kən ˈtɪn ju:]	→ [kən ˈtɪn jʊəs]
	contemptuous	[kən ˈtɛmpt]	→ [kən ˈtɛmp tʃʊəs]

Table 40: stress-repelling suffixes: shift to penultimate syllable

A second group of stress-repelling suffixes leads to a stress shift onto the last-but-two syllable, the antepenultimate [ˌæntipɪˈnʌltɪmət] syllable.

suffix	example	without suffix	with stress shift
-ate	*fascinate*	[fæ sɪ ˈneɪ ʃn̩]	→ [ˈfæs ɪ neɪt]
	differentiate	[ˈdɪf rənt]	→ [dɪ fə ˈren ʃi eɪt]
-ety	*society*	[ˈsəʊ ʃəl]	→ [sə ˈsaɪ ə ti]
	variety	[ˈvɛə ri əs]	→ [və ˈraɪ ə ti]
-ical	*economical*	[iː ˈkɒn ə mi]	→ [iː kə ˈnɒm ɪ kl̩]
	historical	[ˈhɪs tri]	→ [hɪ ˈstɒr ɪ kl̩]
-(i)fy	*specify*	[spɛ ˈsɪf ɪk]	→ [ˈspɛs ɪ faɪ]
	satisfy	[sæ tɪs ˈfæk ʃn̩]	→ [ˈsæt ɪs ˈfaɪ]
-itive	*definitive*	[dɛ fə ˈnɪʃ n̩]	→ [di ˈfɪn ə tɪv]
	intuitive	[ɪn tjuː ˈɪʃ n̩]	→ [ɪn ˈtjuː ə tɪv]
-ity	*possibility*	[ˈpɒs ə bl̩]	→ [pɒ sə ˈbɪl ə ti]
	brutality	[ˈbruː tl̩]	→ [bruː ˈtæl ə ti]
-cracy	*bureaucracy*	[ˈbju rəʊ]	→ [bju ˈrɒk rə si]
	democracy	[ˈdɛm ə kræt]	→ [dɪ ˈmɒk rə si]
-graphy	*orthography*	[ˈɔː θəʊ dɒks]	→ [ɔː ˈθɒg rə fi]
	biography	[ˈbaɪ əʊ pɪk]	→ [baɪ ˈɒg rə fi]
-logy	*biology*	[ˈbaɪ əʊ gæs]	→ [baɪ ˈɒl ə dʒi]
	psychology	[ˈsaɪ kəʊ pæθ]	→ [saɪ ˈkɒl ə dʒi]
-meter	*thermometer*	[ˈθɜː məʊ stæt]	→ [θə ˈmɒm ɪ tə]
	speedometer	[ˈspiːd]	→ [spiː ˈdɒm ɪ tə]

Table 41: stress-repelling suffixes: shift to antepenultimate syllable

Note that in the tables above, it is not always the case that the word containing the stress-shifting suffix developed from the word without the suffix. The tables merely contrast two related words and the impact of a stress-shifting suffix on their pronunciation.

British vs. American Pronunciation

For several words, the British and the American pronunciation standards differ as to which syllable is stressed. For many of these, GA stresses the first syllable, while RP has stress on a later syllable. But there are equally cases where the opposite is true.

	🇬🇧	🇺🇸
cigarette	[sɪgə'rɛt]	['sɪgərɛt]
laboratory	[lə'bɒrətəri]	['læbrətɔːri]
controversy	[kən'trɒvəsi]	['kɑːntrəvɝːsi]
applicable	[ə'plɪkəbl̩]	['æplɪkəbl̩]
inquiry	[ɪn'kwaɪəri]	['ɪnkwəri]
translate	[træns'leɪt]	['trænsleɪt]
research	[ri'sɜːtʃ]	['riːsɝːtʃ]
resource	[ri'zɔːs]	['riːsɔːrs]
ice cream	[ˌaɪs 'kriːm]	['aɪs kriːm]
donate	[dəʊ'neɪt]	['doʊneɪt]
spectator	[spɛk'teɪtə]	['spɛkteɪtɚ]
narrator	[nə'reɪtə]	['næreɪtɚ]
baptize	[bæp'taɪz]	['bæptaɪz]
regulatory	[ˌrɛgju'leɪtəri]	['rɛgjələtɔːri]
adult	['ædʌlt]	[ə'dʌlt]
brochure	['brəʊʃə]	[broʊ'ʃʊr]
garage	['gærɑːʒ]	[gə'rɑːʒ]
harass	['hærəs]	[hə'ræs]
premature	['prɛmətʃə]	[ˌpriːmə'tʊr]
communal	['kɒmjʊnl̩]	[kə'mjuːnl̩]
debut	['deɪbjuː]	[deɪ'bjuː]
fiancé	[fi'ɒnseɪ]	[fiːɑːn'seɪ]

Table 42: stress differences between RP and GA

Exercises

10.1

Transcribe the following words including word stress and sort them into the correct column depending on which syllable is stressed.

yesterday, today, tomorrow, morning, afternoon, July, October, Thursday, Saturday, comprehend, 13, 17, 50, photograph, percentage

'xx	x'x	'xxx	x'xx	xx'x

10.2

Pronounce the following nouns with the correct English stress pattern, especially if the word exists as a loanword in your mother-tongue.

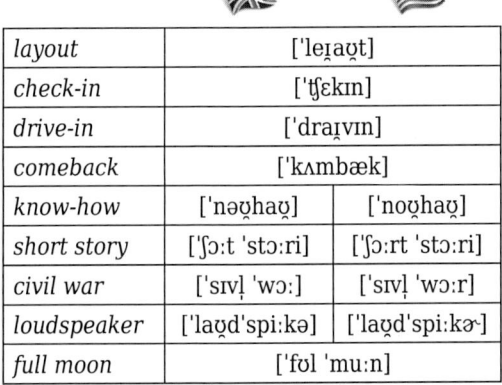

layout	['leɪ̯aʊ̯t]	
check-in	['tʃɛkɪn]	
drive-in	['draɪ̯vɪn]	
comeback	['kʌmbæk]	
know-how	['nəʊ̯haʊ̯]	['noʊ̯haʊ̯]
short story	['ʃɔːt 'stɔːri]	['ʃɔːrt 'stɔːri]
civil war	['sɪvl̩ 'wɔː]	['sɪvl̩ 'wɔːr]
loudspeaker	['laʊ̯d'spiːkə]	['laʊ̯d'spiːkɚ]
full moon	['fʊl 'muːn]	

10.3

Transcribe the following passage from *Heart of Darkness* by Joseph Conrad.

A slight clinking behind me made me turn my head. Six black men advanced in a file, toiling up the path. They walked erect and slow, balancing small baskets full of earth on their heads, and the clink kept time with their footsteps. Black rags were wound round their loins, and the short ends behind wagged to and fro like tails. I could see every rib, the joints of their limbs were like knots in a rope; each had an iron collar on his neck, and all were connected together with a chain whose bights swung between them, rhythmically clinking.

Listen to a recording of the transcription text online at:
www.phonetiker.net/transcript/

10.4

Read the following IPA transcription from *The Picture of Dorian Gray* by Oscar Wilde and write the text orthographically.

 [əz hi wəz tɜːnɪŋ ðə ˈhændl̩ əv ðə ˈdɔː | hɪz ˈaɪ fɛl əpɒn ðə ˈpɔːtrət | bæzl̩ hɔːlwəd həd ˈpeɪntɪd əv hɪm | hi stɑːtɪd ˈbæk | æz ɪf m̩ səˈpraɪz ‖ ɪn ðə ˈdɪm ərɛstɪd ˈlaɪt | ðət strʌɡəld θruː ðə kriːmkʌləd ˈsɪlk blaɪndz | ðə ˈfeɪs əpɪəd tə hɪm | tə bi ə lɪtl̩ ˈtʃeɪndʒd ‖ ði ɪkˈsprɛʃn̩ lʊkt ˈdɪfrənt ‖ wʌn wʊd həv ˈsɛd | ðət ðɛə wəz ə tʌtʃ əv ˈkruːəlti ɪn ðə maʊθ ‖ ɪt wəz sɜːtn̩li ˈstreɪndʒ]

 [əz hi wəz tɝːnɪŋ ðə ˈhændl̩ əv ðə ˈdɔːr | hɪz ˈaɪ fɛl əpɑːn ðə ˈpɔːrtrət | bæzl̩ hɔːlwərd həd ˈpeɪntɪd əv hɪm | hi stɑːrtɪd ˈbæk | æz ɪf m̩ səˈpraɪz ‖ ɪn ðə ˈdɪm ərɛstɪd ˈlaɪt | ðət strʌɡəld θruː ðə kriːmkʌlərd ˈsɪlk blaɪndz | ðə ˈfeɪs əpɪrd tə hɪm | tə bi ə lɪtl̩ ˈtʃeɪndʒd ‖ ði ɪkˈsprɛʃn̩ lʊkt ˈdɪfrənt ‖ wʌn wʊd həv ˈsɛd | ðət ðɛr wəz ə tʌtʃ əv ˈkruːəlti ɪn ðə maʊθ ‖ ɪt wəz sɝːtn̩li ˈstreɪndʒ]

Listen to a recording of the transcription text online at:
www.phonetiker.net/transcript/

11 Intonation: Tonality and Tonicity
[ɪntəʊˈneɪʃn̩ | təʊˈnæləti ənd təʊˈnɪsəti]

Intonation is the change in pitch associated with an utterance. In the example
"Tomorrow? – Tomorrow.", the first sentence is a question, the second one an
answer. When spoken aloud, this can also be heard even though the phonetic
transcription is the same for both utterances: [təˈmɒrəʊ ‖ təˈmɑːrəʊ]. This
illustrates that, in addition to the segmental level (the succession of phonemes),
there is another level contributing to communication stretching over bigger
units than the individual phonemes: the suprasegmental level. It is the fact
that one utterance is spoken with rising, the other one with falling intonation
which makes them a question or a statement respectively.

Intonation carries not only linguistic but also paralinguistic meaning. On
the linguistic level, intonation reflects the syntactic structure of a sentence.
What is indicated with punctuation marks in written discourse can often be
heard in spoken interactions. It also contributes to the understanding of
discourse, by providing cues which information is already known (theme)
and which is new (rheme).

On the paralinguistic level, intonation communicates the feelings and
intentions of a speaker. Whether a speaker is friendly, uninterested, determined;
whether they are sarcastic or ironic – all of these attitudes can be reflected
in intonation.

Once speakers have decided what they want to say and have looked for
the appropriate words that will constitute the segmental level, they are faced
with three tasks on the suprasegmental level: the speech flow must be broken
down into units; within these units, some words will be stressed while others
remain unstressed; and finally, it has to be decided whether intonation rises,
falls or remains level. These three tasks are referred to as tonality, tonicity
and tone.

tonality	tonicity	tone
grouping the speech flow into intonation phrases	placement of stressed syllables within an intonation phrase	choice of a specific intonation pattern for the tonic syllable

Figure 21: the three 'Ts' in intonation

Tonality

Tonality is the division of the speech flow into units. These units are called intonation phrases. An intonation phrase is a unit over which one intonation pattern is realised. The question of how big or small an intonation phrase is cannot be easily answered. It depends on the individual speaker and such criteria as how fast or slowly they speak. Generally, it can, however, be observed that intonation phrases coincide with sense units. In other words, what belongs together is spoken together.

Tonality can alter the sense of an utterance. If a string of phonemes is spoken as one or two intonation phrases, can lead to a difference in meaning. Considering numbers, for instance, the grouping into intonation phrases can yield different results. The string [twɛnti faɪv sɪksti tuː], as an example, is ambiguous. Only once it has been grouped into intonation phrases, does it become clear what number is meant.

[twɛnti 'faɪv | sɪksti 'tuː]	= 25 62
[twɛnti 'faɪv | 'sɪksti | 'tuː]	= 25 60 2
['twɛnti | 'faɪv | sɪksti 'tuː]	= 20 5 62
['twɛnti | 'faɪv | 'sɪksti | 'tuː]	= 20 5 60 2

Table 43: example for tonality

Tonality mirrors the syntactic structure of an utterance. One example where this becomes apparent are relative clauses which can either be restrictive or non-restrictive. In a restrictive clause, the relative clause helps identify the referent while, in a non-restrictive relative clause, it merely provides additional information. The sentence *"The children(,) who cried(,) got a lolly."* has a different meaning depending on whether the relative clause is restrictive. With a non-restrictive clause, the sentence states that the children got a lolly and the relative clause provides the additional information that the children were crying. With a restrictive clause, some children cried, while others did not and only the ones who cried got a lolly. Tonality makes this difference audible.

The children who cried got a lolly. (restrictive) [ðə ʧɪldrən hu 'kraɪd ǀ gɒt ə 'lɒli]	*The children, who cried, got a lolly.* (non-restrictive) [ðə 'ʧɪldrən ǀ hu 'kraɪd ǀ gɒt ə 'lɒli]

Table 44: tonality and relative clauses

Sentences containing an adverb in final position are sometimes ambiguous. The adverb can either modify the verb and describe how the action was carried out or it can function as a sentence adverbial and modify the sentence as a whole. This ambiguity is resolved through tonality, where the utterance is either spoken as one or two intonation phrases.

He doesn't do it normally. ("in a normal way") [hi dʌznt du ɪt 'nɔːməli]	*He doesn't do it, normally.* ("under normal circumstances") [hi dʌznt 'duː ɪt ǀ 'nɔːməli]

Table 45: tonality and adverbials

Tonicity

Tonicity means the stress placement within an intonation phrase. When looking at word stress, it can be observed that, in any word which has more than one syllable, there are syllables that are stressed and others that remain unstressed. The same is true for intonation phrases where there is also a succession of stressed and unstressed syllables.

How many and which syllables are stressed within an intonation phrase largely depends on the individual speaker and the speech situation. But, as for tonality, predictions can be made. In the sentence *"I'm going home now."*, most speakers would probably stress ⟨I'm⟩ and ⟨home⟩, leaving the remaining syllables unstressed. The rhythmic structure of this sentence could hence be represented as 'x x x 'x x (with 'x' standing for one syllable). An alternation of stressed and unstressed syllables can be observed.

All languages have rhythm, a pattern of how syllables follow one after another. In English, as in many Germanic and Slavonic languages, rhythm appears to be based on the succession of stressed syllables. Such languages are called stress-timed languages. In stress-timed languages, the rhythmic pattern is established by counting from one stressed syllable to the next stressed one and adjusting anything that lies in-between accordingly. That means that roughly the same amount of time will elapse from one stressed syllable to the next stressed one. Unstressed syllables that lie in-between must be shortened in order to fit this rhythmic pattern.

The three examples below all contain the syllable [mæ] in three different words and the word [hɪə ‖ hɪr]. In all three examples, it would be these syllables that receive stress. However, the examples differ in how many unstressed syllables lie in-between: there are either none, one or two unstressed syllables between the two stressed ones. Still, as English is a stress-timed language, the same amount of time will elapse from [mæ] to [hɪə ‖ hɪr]. But that means that the [mæ] in ⟨man⟩ can be much longer than the [mæ] in ⟨manor⟩ and that the [mæ] in ⟨manager⟩ must be shortest. Also the unstressed syllables must be heavily reduced, in order to fit the stress-timed rhythm.

x	'x		'x	x	'x	x	'x	x	'x	x	x	x	'x
[ðə 'mænz 'hɪə̯]				[ðə 'mæ.nəz 'hɪə̯]				[ðə 'mæ.nɪ.dʒəz 'hɪə̯]					
the man's here				*the manor's here*				*the manager's here*					

Table 46: illustration of syllable timing

Syllable-timed languages, on the other hand, show a different rhythm. Many Romance or Indian languages are syllable-timed. In such languages, stressed syllables do not play a role for the rhythmic pattern. Rather the same amount of time will elapse from one syllable to the next, regardless of whether it is stressed or not. But that means that the time from one stressed syllable to the next stressed one is different.

Since English as a stress-timed language establishes its rhythm on the basis of an equal distribution of stressed syllables, two adjacent words may receive stress, but not three. This is called the three accent rule. For instance, in the sentence ⟨She is very old.⟩ both ⟨very⟩ and ⟨old⟩ would be equally stressed (level stress): [ʃiz 'vɛri 'əʊ̯ld]. If, however, another word is added, one stress must be dropped. So (She is not very old.) would be spoken as [ʃiz 'nɒt vɛri 'əʊld] or (She is a very old cat.) becomes [ʃiz ə 'vɛri əʊld 'kæt], in order to re-establish the stress-timed rhythm.

Tonicity, the stress placement within an intonation phrase, has a communicative function in that it is the most newsworthy information which speakers stress. In the above example "I'm going home now.", it was (I'm) and (home) that were stressed, which are essentially the most important words in that sentence. English is an SPO language: the subject says who or what the sentence is about, while predicate and object finally express what happened to the subject. Because of this structure, the most newsworthy information tends to occur towards the end of a sentence and therefore also the main or tonic stress in an intonation phrase tends to occur there.

Theoretically, any word of a sentence can be stressed. However, moving the tonic stress to an earlier word creates a marked tonicity with contrastive stress. It is called contrastive stress because the word that is stressed stands in contrast to something else which is not explicitly said but implied by the contrastive stress.

I cannot sell you that house.	
['aɪ kænɒt sɛl ju ðæt haʊs]	...but someone else might.
[aɪ 'kænɒt sɛl ju ðæt haʊs]	...I really can't.
[aɪ kænɒt 'sɛl ju ðæt haʊs]	...but you could rent it.
[aɪ kænɒt sɛl 'ju: ðæt haʊs]	...but to someone else.
[aɪ kænɒt sɛl ju 'ðæt haʊs]	...but there is another one.
[aɪ kænɒt sɛl ju ðæt 'haʊs]	...but you can have a flat.

Table 47: contrastive stress

Exercises

11.1

Transcribe the following sentences and decide which words would be stressed with neutral tonicity.

a) *When I came home, the TV was still running.*
b) *No student must leave the room.*
c) *Put it on the table over there.*
d) *I don't think I can.*
e) *I'm Frank. And what's your name?*
f) *Should we buy the new one?*

11.2

Transcribe the following passage from *The Strange Case of Dr. Jekyll and Mr. Hyde* by Robert Louis Stevenson.

He put the glass to his lips and drank at one gulp. A cry followed; he reeled, staggered, clutched at the table and held on, staring with injected eyes, gasping with open mouth; and as I looked there came, I thought, a change – he seemed to swell – his face became suddenly black and the features seemed to melt and alter – and the next moment, I had sprung to my feet and leaped back against the wall, my arm raised to shield me from that prodigy, my mind submerged in terror.

 Listen to a recording of the transcription text online at: www.phonetiker.net/transcript/

11.3

Read the following IPA transcription from *Dubliners* by James Joyce and write the text orthographically.

 [fju: pi:pḷ 'pɑːst ‖ ðə 'mæn aʊ̯t əv ðə lɑːst 'haʊ̯s | 'pɑːst ɒn hɪz weɪ̯ 'həʊ̯m | ʃi hɜːd hɪz 'fʊtstɛps | klækɪŋ əlɒŋ ðə 'kɒŋkriːt peɪ̯vmənt | ənd 'ɑːftəwədz | krʌntʃɪŋ ɒn ðə 'sɪndə pɑːθ | bifɔː ðə nju: rɛd 'haʊ̯zɪz ‖ wʌn 'taɪ̯m | ðɛə̯ ju:st tə bi ə 'fiːld ðɛə̯ | ɪn wɪtʃ ðeɪ̯ ju:st tə 'pleɪ̯ ɛvri iːvnɪŋ | wɪð ʌðə piːpḷz 'tʃɪldrən ‖ ðɛn ə mæn frəm bɛl'fɑːst bɔːt ðə 'fiːld | ənd bɪlt 'haʊ̯zɪz ɪn ɪt | nɒt laɪ̯k 'ðɛə̯ lɪtḷ braʊ̯n haʊ̯zɪz | bət braɪ̯t 'brɪk haʊ̯zɪz | wɪð ʃaɪ̯nɪŋ 'ruːfs]

 [fju: pi:pḷ 'pæst ‖ ðə 'mæn aʊ̯t əv ðə læst 'haʊ̯s | 'pæst ɑːn hɪz weɪ̯ 'hoʊ̯m | ʃi hɜ˞ːd hɪz 'fʊtstɛps | klækɪŋ əlɔːŋ ðə 'kɑːnkriːt peɪ̯vmənt | ənd 'æftə˞wə˞dz | krʌntʃɪŋ ɑːn ðə 'sɪndə˞ pæθ | bifɔːr ðə nu: rɛd 'haʊ̯zɪz ‖ wʌn 'taɪ̯m | ðɛr ju:st tə bi ə 'fiːld ðɛr | ɪn wɪtʃ ðeɪ̯ ju:st tə 'pleɪ̯ ɛvri iːvnɪŋ | wɪθ ʌðə˞ piːpḷz 'tʃɪldrən ‖ ðɛn ə mæn frəm 'bɛlfæst bɔːt ðə 'fiːld | ənd bɪlt 'haʊ̯zɪz ɪn ɪt | nɑːt laɪ̯k 'ðɛr lɪtḷ braʊ̯n haʊ̯zɪz | bət braɪ̯t 'brɪk haʊ̯zɪz | wɪθ ʃaɪ̯nɪŋ 'ruːfs]

Listen to a recording of the transcription text online at:
www.phonetiker.net/transcript/

12 Intonation: Tone
[ɪntəʊ̯ˈneɪ̯ʃn̩ | ˈtəʊ̯n]

The word "intonation" includes the word tone. Indeed, besides grouping the speech flow with the right tonality and finding a fitting rhythm as tonicity, speakers need to decide on a tone. Tone is the variation in pitch on the last accented syllable within an intonation phrase. The tone of a syllable can rise, fall or remain level.

Languages exist where tone creates lexical differences. Depending on whether a syllable is pronounced with high or low, rising or falling pitch, a word has a different meaning. In Mandarin Chinese, for example, the word (mā) with a level tone means (mother). Spoken with a rising tone (má), it is a different word and means (hemp). If the word is pronounced with a fall-rise (mǎ), the word is (horse). (mà) with a falling tone, on the other hand, means (scold).

English does not use tone for creating lexical contrasts. Nevertheless, tone has linguistic meaning as it signals sentence type, and also whether an element is a main or subordinate clause. In English, there are several tones that can be subdivided into falling and non-falling tones. Intonation contours are drawn between two horizontal lines that represent the speaking range of a person and show the pitch for the individual syllables of an utterance.

Falling Tones

Falling tones signal finality and independence. Saying that statements are pronounced with falling intonation and questions with a rising one is too simplistic. Yet it is true that falling intonation is the default tone for statements and other sentences, such as exclamations and imperatives, all of which have assertive character. Furthermore, while subordinate clauses are pronounced with non-falling tones, elements that are independent and can stand on their own show falling intonation.

English knows three falling tones: the low fall, the high fall and the rise-fall. All falling tones end in the lower speaking range. However, while the low fall drops from mid to low, the high fall starts high. The rise-fall, on the other hand, starts about mid, rises to high and falls to low. Before a falling tone, there is often an upstep in intonation, i.e. speakers go a little higher before their intonation finally drops.

Figure 22: falling tones: low fall, high fall, rise-fall

Non-Falling Tones

Non-falling tones are associated with non-finality and dependence. An utterance which is spoken with a non-fall is either a dependent element and it is signalled through intonation that the sentence will still go on or it prompts the interlocutor for a reaction as, for instance, in a yes/no-question.

The four non-falling tones in English are the low rise, the high rise, the fall-rise and the level tone, which have different start and end positions. While the low rise starts low and rises to mid, the high rise starts at about mid-level and rises into high register. The fall-rise starts quite high, drops to low and comes back up to mid. A level tone remains at mid-level. Before a rise, often a downstep can be heard, where speakers go a little lower before their pitch rises.

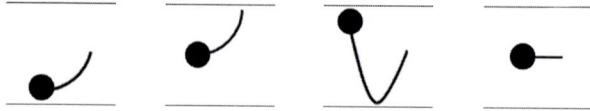

Figure 23: non-falling tones: low rise, high rise, fall-rise and level

Listen to recordings of nuclear tones online at:
www.phonetiker.net/transcript/

Structure of Intonation Phrases

An intonation phrase can contain several stressed syllables with unstressed syllables in-between. It is the last of the stressed syllables that carries the main stress where the tone is realised. Therefore, this syllable is also called the tonic and it forms the nucleus of the intonation phrase.

The nucleus is usually one of the last syllables within an intonation phrase. Any unstressed syllables that follow the nucleus are called the tail. If an intonation phrase contains a tail, the tone that was started on the nucleus is stretched over the tail. Thus, if the nucleus contains a falling tone, intonation keeps on falling or remains low over the tail. If the tone is a rise, the intonation pattern keeps on rising or remains high.

Syllables before the nucleus are referred to as the head. If the head contains further stressed syllables, the first one of these is the onset. The onset shows an upstep: it is higher in pitch than the syllables which precede it. Any unstressed syllables before the onset are called pre-head.

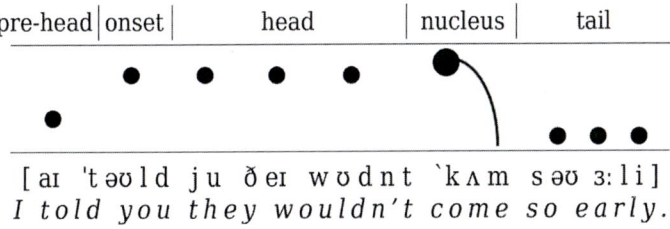

Figure 24: structure of an intonation phrase

Sentence Types

Languages distinguish between different kinds of sentences, such as statements or questions. Besides word order signalling sentence type, e.g. when the auxiliary precedes the subject in questions, intonation also reflects this. There are sentence types where virtually only one pattern, rise or fall, is possible. For the majority of sentence types, several tones can be heard but there is a default one which is the preferred and neutral choice.

To say that questions are spoken with rising intonation is false. In fact, it is only questions that can be answered with either yes or no (yes/no-questions) that exhibit rising intonation. Even these can be pronounced with a fall in order to sound more insistent. The default pattern for questions that start with a question word (wh-questions) is falling, though speakers sometimes employ a rising intonation in order to sound friendlier and more welcoming. Alternative questions, such as "Would you like tea or coffee?", are always spoken with a fall on the last element. Question tags are spoken with rising intonation to indicate they are intended as a real question. Otherwise they show a falling tone.

All other sentence types have a falling tone as their default pattern. When spoken with a rising tone, a command can sound friendlier. For instance, "Come in!" with a rise instead of a fall sounds more encouraging to the addressee. Statements can be made to sound like a question by employing a rising tone without marking them explicitly as a question by reversing subject and auxiliary.

statements	default: falling fall-rise signals an implication rise in declarative questions or uptalk
commands	default: falling rise as more encouraging fall-rise in warnings
exclamations	always falling
wh-questions	default: falling rise as a more friendly question
yes/no-questions	default: rising fall heard as insistent
alternative questions	always falling rise heard as yes/no-question
tag-questions	falling in rhetorical questions rising in genuine questions

Table 48: default intonation of different sentence types

Dependent and Independent Elements

Complex sentences contain in addition to the main clause also subordinate elements. The main clause is an independent element and pronounced with an intonation pattern as outlined above. Subordinate clauses and phrases, on the other hand, are dependent elements and therefore always pronounced with a non-falling intonation contour.

Which type of non-falling tone occurs in the subordinate element, depends on its position within the sentence. If it occurs before the main clause, it will be pronounced with a fall-rise. Enumerations are also spoken with fall-rises on all elements except the last, which has falling intonation. On the other hand, if the dependent element comes last in the sentence, it is pronounced with a rising tone.

Before breakfast, I won't start.	*I won't start, before breakfast.*
(dependent first: fall-rise)	(depending last: rise)
[bifɔ: ˅brɛkfəst | aɪ̯ wəʊ̯nt ⟍stɑːt]	[aɪ̯ wəʊ̯nt ⟍stɑːt | bifɔ: ˊbrɛkfəst]

Table 49: tone in dependent elements

Expressiveness

The intonation of an utterance conveys linguistic information, such as sentence type, sentence structure and what information is new or given. Furthermore, intonation serves an expressive function, in that it encodes the speaker's attitudes and feelings.

While it is true that the choice of tone can carry expressive information, it proves difficult to establish a systematic between an intonation pattern and its interpretation. Generally it can be said that tones which enter the high register are more expressive and carry emotional overtones.

Exercises

12.1

Transcribe the following sentences, marking tonality and tonicity. Indicate tone as falling [ˋ], rising [ˊ] or as a fall-rise [ˇ] before the tonic syllable.

    a)   Where do you think you're going?
    b)   After he left, the room was much quieter.
    c)   Such a beautiful dog!
    d)   Are you coming?
    e)   Are you coming or going?
    f)   Come in and leave your shoes on.

12.2

Although the following sentences contain the same words, there can be different readings. In spoken language, do the sentences differ in tonality, tonicity or tone?

    a)   *And he will do it, right?*
          And he will do it right?
    b)   *He'll be twenty-five in May.* ("It's in May he'll turn 25.")
          He'll be twenty-five in May. ("It's his 25th birthday in May.")
    c)   *That's not fair.*
          That's not fair?
    d)   *Would you like tea or coffee?* ("Would you like a hot drink?")
          Would you like tea or coffee? ("Do you want coffee or tea?")
    e)   *I thought you would eat it.* ("I knew you would eat it.")
          I thought you would eat it. ("I'm surprised you're not eating.")
    f)   *She dressed and fed the baby.* ("She dressed the child.")
          She dressed and fed the baby. ("She dressed herself.")

12.3

Transcribe the following passage from *Through the Looking-Glass* by Lewis Carroll.

However, the egg only got larger and larger, and more and more human: when she had come within a few yards of it, she saw that it had eyes and a nose and mouth; and when she had come close to it, she saw clearly that it was Humpty Dumpty himself. Humpty Dumpty was sitting with his legs crossed, like a Turk, on the top of a high wall – such a narrow one that Alice quite wondered how he could keep his balance – and, as his eyes were steadily fixed in the opposite direction, and he didn't take the least notice of her, she thought he must be a stuffed figure after all.

Listen to a recording of the transcription text online at:
www.phonetiker.net/transcript/

12.4

Read the following IPA transcription from *The Pit and the Pendulum* by Edgan Alan Poe and write the text orthographically.

[lʊkɪŋ ˈʌpwəd | aɪ səveɪd ðə ˈsiːlɪŋ əv maɪ prɪzn̩ ‖ wɒt aɪ ðen ˈsɔː | kənˈfaʊndɪd ənd əˈmeɪzd miː ‖ ðə swiːp əv ðə ˈpɛndjʊləm | həd ɪnˈkriːst ɪn ɪkˈstɛnt | baɪ nɪəˌli ə ˈjɑːd ‖ əz ə næt͡ʃərəl ˈkɒnsɪkwəns | ɪts vəˈlɒsəti | wəz ˈɔːlsəʊ mʌt͡ʃ greɪtə ‖ bət wɒt ˈmeɪnli dɪstɜːbd miː | wəz ði aɪˈdɪə | ðæt ɪt həd pəsɛptəbli diˈsɛndɪd ‖ ðə vaɪˌbreɪʃn̩ əv ðə ˈpɛndjʊləm | wəz ət raɪt ˈæŋglz | tə maɪ ˈlɛŋθ ‖ aɪ sɔː ðət ðə ˈkrɛzn̩t wəz diˈzaɪnd | tə krɒs ðə ˈriːd͡ʒn̩ əv ðə ˈhɑːt]

[lʊkɪŋ ˈʌpwɚd | aɪ səˈveɪd ðə ˈsiːlɪŋ əv maɪ prɪzn̩ ‖ wʌt aɪ ðen ˈsɔː | kənˈfaʊndɪd ənd əˈmeɪzd miː ‖ ðə swiːp əv ðə ˈpɛndʒələm | həd ɪnˈkriːst ɪn ɪkˈstɛnt | baɪ nɪrli ə ˈjɑːrd ‖ əz ə næt͡ʃərəl ˈkɑːnsəkwəns | ɪts vəˈlɑːsəti | wəz ˈɔːlsəʊ mʌt͡ʃ greɪtɚ ‖ bət wʌt ˈmeɪnli dɪstɜːbd miː | wəz ði aɪˈdiːə | ðæt ɪt həd pɚsɛptəbli diˈsɛndɪd ‖ ðə vaɪˌbreɪʃn̩ əv ðə ˈpɛndʒələm | wəz ət raɪt ˈæŋglz | tə maɪ ˈlɛŋθ ‖ aɪ sɔː ðət ðə ˈkrɛsn̩t wəz diˈzaɪnd | tə krɔːs ðə ˈriːd͡ʒn̩ əv ðə ˈhɑːrt]

Listen to a recording of the transcription text online at:
www.phonetiker.net/transcript/

List of IPA Symbols
['lɪst əv aɪ̯ pi: eɪ̯ 'sɪmbl̩z]

IPA symbols as used in the transcription system of the respective language.

IPA	description	English	German	French
a	low central unrounded vowel	—	kann	plat
aː	low central unrounded vowel	—	Bad	—
ae̯	closing diphthong	—	mein	—
aɪ̯	closing diphthong	my	—	—
ao̯	closing diphthong	—	Frau	—
aʊ̯	closing diphthong	how	—	—
ɑː	low back unrounded vowel	father	—	—
ɑ̃	low back unrounded nasal vowel	—	—	sans
ɒ	higher low back rounded vowel	got RP	—	—
ɐ	higher low central unrounded vowel	—	bitter	—
æ	higher low front unrounded vowel	trap	—	—
b	bilabial lenis plosive	be	bei	bon
β	bilabial lenis fricative	Spanish: lava		
c	palatal fortis plosive	Turkish: köyün		
ç	palatal fortis fricative	—	ich	—
d	alveolar lenis plosive	do	da	dans
dʒ	postalveolar lenis affricate	age	—	—
ð	dental lenis fricative	this	—	—
eː	upper mid front unrounded vowel	—	zehn	chez
eɪ̯	closing diphthong	they	—	—
ə	mid central unrounded vowel	ago	bitte	que
əʊ̯	closing diphthong	so RP	—	—
ɚ	rhotic mid central unrounded vowel	better GA	—	—

IPA	description	English	German	French
ɛ	lower mid front unrounded vowel	—	nett	quel
ɛ	mid front unrounded vowel	get	—	—
ɛə̯	centring diphthong	there ᴿᴾ	—	—
ɛ̃	lower mid front unrounded nasal vowel	—	—	**un**
ɜ:	mid central unrounded vowel	nurse ᴿᴾ	—	—
ɝ:	rhotic mid central unrounded vowel	nurse ᴳᴬ	—	—
f	labiodental fortis fricative	fun	frei	froid
ɡ	velar lenis plosive	**g**o	**g**eht	**g**are
h	glottal fortis fricative	**h**ere	**h**eute	
ɥ	labial-palatal lenis approximant	—	—	**h**uit
i:	high front unrounded vowel	see	ihm	—
i	high front unrounded vowel	happy	Filet	ils
ɪ	lower high front-centr. unrounded vowel	it	in	—
ɪə̯	centring diphthong	here ᴿᴾ	—	—
j	palatal lenis approximant	**y**es	**j**a	fi**ll**e
ʝ	palatal lenis fricative	Dutch: **g**oed		
ɟ	palatal lenis plosive	Turkish: **g**üneş		
k	velar fortis plosive	cat	Kind	**qu**i
l	alveolar lenis lateral approximant	love	links	long
ɫ	velarised alveolar lenis lateral approx.	ca**ll**	—	—
ɬ	alveolar fortis lateral fricative	Welsh: **ll**an		
ʎ	palatal lenis lateral approximant	Italian: fami**gl**ia		
m	bilabial lenis nasal	**m**eet	**m**it	**m**oi
ɱ	labiodental lenis nasal	co**m**fort	Se**n**f	—
n	alveolar lenis nasal	**n**o	**n**ein	**n**on
ŋ	velar lenis nasal	ri**ng**	Di**ng**	parki**ng**
ɲ	palatal lenis nasal	—	—	co**gn**ac

IPA	description	English	German	French
oː	upper mid back rounded vowel	—	so	eau
oʊ̯	closing diphthong	so GA	—	—
ɔ	lower mid back rounded vowel	—	oft	pomme
ɔː	mid back rounded vowel	caught	—	—
ɔ̃	lower mid back rounded nasal vowel	—	—	son
ɔɪ̯	closing diphthong	joy	—	—
ɔø̯	closing diphthong	—	neu	—
øː	upper mid front rounded vowel	—	schön	peu
œ	lower mid front rounded vowel	—	können	fleur
p	bilabial fortis plosive	pen	Paar	père
ɹ	postalveolar lenis approximant	right	—	—
ɻ	retroflex lenis approximant	American accents: right		
R	uvular lenis trill	in French often for [ʁ]		
ʁ	velar-uvular lenis fricative	—	rechts	rire
ɾ	alveolar lenis tap	see below		
s	alveolar fortis fricative	see	Kuss	se
ʃ	postalveolar fortis fricative	she	schon	chaud
t	alveolar fortis plosive	tea	Tag	toi
tʃ	postalveolar fortis affricate	church	—	—
ts	alveolar fortis affricate	—	Zeit	—
θ	dental fortis fricative	thing	—	—
uː	high back rounded vowel	shoe	Kuh	—
u	high back rounded vowel	you	Duell	sous
ʊ	lower high back-centr. rounded vowel	put	muss	—
ʊə̯	centring diphthong	cure RP	—	—
v	labiodental lenis fricative	very	wer	vers
ʌ	higher low central unrounded vowel	cut	—	—

IPA	description	English	German	French
w	labial-velar lenis approximant	were	—	oui
ʍ	labial-velar fortis fricative	some English accents: why		
x	velar fortis fricative	—	Nacht	—
y:	high front rounded vowel	—	für	tu
ʏ	lower high front-centr. rounded vowel	—	Müll	—
z	alveolar lenis fricative	zero	sie	rose
ʒ	postalveolar lenis fricative	vision	Garage	jour
ʔ	glottal fortis plosive	see below		
ˈ	stress	[ʌnˈtru:]	[ˈʔʊnvaːʁ]	—
ˌ	syllabic	[piːpl̩]	[ʃliːsn̩]	—
̯	non-syllabic	[hɪə̯]	[ʔeː ̯ɐ̯]	—
̥	voiceless	[pl̥iːs]	[kg̊aːn]	[ab̥sã]
̬	voiced	[bɛt̬ɚ]	—	[ʃak̬ʒuʁ]
̞	lowered (more open)	[drɛ̞s]	[vɛ̞ɐt]	[etɛ̞]
̝	raised (more close)	[θɔ̝ːt]	[kɛ̝zə]	[etɛ̝]
̟	advanced (further front)	[k̟iː]	[ka̟m]	[dy̟t]
̠	retracted (further back)	[k̠ɑː]	[a̠ʁm]	[k̠ɔʁ]
̈	centralised	[skü:l]	[tsü]	[fɔ̈ʁ]
̪	dental	[mʌn̪θ]	—	—
̚	unreleased	[wɒt̚]	[ʔʊnt̚]	—
ʰ	aspirated	[pʰʊt]	[tʰeː]	—
ʷ	labialised	[ʃʷu:]	[ʃʷʊltɐ]	[dʷø]
ⁿ	nasal release	[bʌtⁿn̩]	[hatⁿn̩]	—
ˡ	lateral release	[kætˡl̩]	[mantˡl̩]	—

Table 50: list of IPA symbols

[ʔ] – In German, every word starting with a vowel actually starts with a glottal stop, e.g. ⟨ein⟩ [ʔaẹn]. In British English, word-final, sometimes intervocalic [t] is often substituted by a glottal stop, e.g. ⟨but⟩ [bʌʔ].

[ɾ] – dialectal variation of ⟨r⟩, e.g. in Scottish English or Bavarian German. In American English, often a substitute for intervocalic [t], e.g. ⟨better⟩ [beɾɚ].

In French, vowel length is not transcribed as it is not phonemic.

Non-IPA Symbols

In older transcriptions, other symbols may appear which are not part of the IPA standard. Their use should be discontinued in favour of IPA.

Non-IPA symbol	IPA equivalent
[š]	[ʃ]
[ž]	[ʒ]
[č]	[tʃ]
[ǰ] [ǯ] [ǧ]	[dʒ]
[ŋ]	[ṇ]
[ʋ] [ʋ] [ɷ]	[ʊ]
[ɩ]	[ɪ]
[aw]	[aʊ̯]
[ay] [aj]	[aɪ̯]
[oy] [oj]	[ɔɪ̯]

Table 51: non-IPA symbols

Solutions to Exercises
[səˈluːʃn̩z tu ˈɛksəsaɪ̯zɪz]

1.1

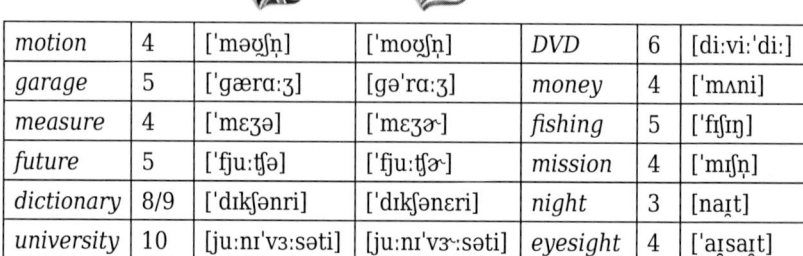

motion	4	[ˈməʊ̯ʃn̩]	[ˈmoʊ̯ʃn̩]	DVD	6	[diːviːˈdiː]
garage	5	[ˈgæraːʒ]	[gəˈraːʒ]	money	4	[ˈmʌni]
measure	4	[ˈmɛʒə]	[ˈmɛʒɚ]	fishing	5	[ˈfɪʃɪŋ]
future	5	[ˈfjuːtʃə]	[ˈfjuːtʃɚ]	mission	4	[ˈmɪʃn̩]
dictionary	8/9	[ˈdɪkʃənri]	[ˈdɪkʃənɛri]	night	3	[naɪt]
university	10	[juːnɪˈvɜːsəti]	[juːnɪˈvɜˑsəti]	eyesight	4	[ˈaɪ̯saɪ̯t]

1.3

The Adventures of Tom Sawyer by Mark Twain

[ˈtɒm əpɪə̯d ɒn ðə ˈsaɪ̯dwɔːk | wɪð ə ˈbʌkɪt əv ˈwaɪ̯twɒʃ | ənd ə lɒŋhændl̩d ˈbrʌʃ ‖ hi səˈveɪ̯d ðə ˈfɛns | ənd ɔːl ˈglædnəs ˈlɛft hɪm | ənd ə diːp ˈmɛlənkəli | sɛtl̩d ˈdaʊ̯n əpɒn hɪz ˈspɪrɪt ‖ θɜːti ˈjɑːdz əv ˈbɔːd fɛns | naɪn fiːt ˈhaɪ̯ | laɪ̯f tə ˈhɪm siːmd ˈhɒləʊ̯ | ənd ɪgˈzɪstəns bʌt ə ˈbɜːdn̩ ‖ ˈsaɪ̯ɪŋ | hi dɪpt hɪz ˈbrʌʃ | ənd ˈpɑːst ɪt əlɒŋ ðə tɒpməʊ̯st ˈplæŋk | rɪˈpiːtɪd ði ɒpəˈreɪ̯ʃn̩ | dɪd ɪt əˈgɛn | kəmˈpɛə̯d ði ɪnsɪgnɪfɪkənt ˈwaɪ̯twɒʃt striːk | wɪð ðə fɑː riːˈtʃɪŋ ˈkɒntɪnənt | əv ˈʌnwaɪ̯twɒʃt fɛns | ənd sæt ˈdaʊ̯n ɒn ə ˈtriː bɒks | dɪsˈkʌrɪdʒd]

[ˈtɑːm əpɪrd ɑːn ðə ˈsaɪ̯dwɔːk | wɪθ ə ˈbʌkət əv ˈwaɪ̯twɑːʃ | ənd ə lɔːŋhændl̩d ˈbrʌʃ ‖ hi səˈveɪ̯d ðə ˈfɛns | ənd ɔːl ˈglædnəs ˈlɛft hɪm | ənd ə diːp ˈmɛlənkɑːli | sɛtl̩d ˈdaʊ̯n əpɑːn hɪz ˈspɪrət ‖ θɜˑti ˈjɑːrdz əv ˈbɔːrd fɛns | naɪn fiːt ˈhaɪ̯ | laɪ̯f tə ˈhɪm siːmd ˈhɑːloʊ̯ | ənd ɪgˈzɪstəns bʌt ə ˈbɜˑdn̩ ‖ ˈsaɪ̯ɪŋ | hi dɪpt hɪz ˈbrʌʃ | ənd ˈpæst ɪt əlɔːŋ ðə tɑːpmoʊ̯st ˈplæŋk | rɪˈpiːtɪd ði ɑːpəˈreɪ̯ʃn̩ | dɪd ɪt əˈgɛn | kəmˈpɛrd ði ɪnsɪgnɪfɪkənt ˈwaɪ̯twɑːʃt striːk | wɪθ ðə fɑːr riːtʃɪŋ ˈkɑːntənənt | əv ˈʌnwaɪ̯twɑːʃt fɛns | ənd sæt ˈdaʊ̯n ɑːn ə ˈtriː bɑːks | dɪsˈkɜˑrɪdʒd]

2.1

judge	[ʤ]	*house*	[s]	*television*	[ʒ]
his	[z]	*through*	[θ]	*resolve*	[z]
live	[v]	*because*	[z]	*future*	[ʧ]
sister	[s]	*method*	[θ]	*choose*	[z]
further	[ð]	*sure*	[ʃ]	*large*	[ʤ]

2.2

e.g. ⟨pair, pear⟩ - [pɛə̯ ‖ pɛr], ⟨cent, scent, sent⟩ - [sɛnt], ⟨waste, waist⟩ - [weɪ̯st], ⟨I, eye⟩ - [aɪ̯], ⟨by, buy, bye⟩ - [baɪ̯], ⟨right, rite, write⟩ - [raɪ̯t], ⟨wear, where⟩ - [wɛə̯ ‖ wɛr]

in RP only: ⟨pore, paw, poor⟩ - [pɔː], ⟨caught, court⟩ - [kɔːt]

2.4

The Time Machine by H. G. Wells

🇬🇧 [aɪ̯ əm ə'freɪ̯d aɪ̯ kænɒt kən'veɪ̯ | ðə pɪkjuːlɪə̯ sɛn'seɪ̯ʃn̩z əv 'taɪm trævəlɪŋ ‖ ðeɪ̯ ɑːr ɪk'sɛsɪvli ʌn'plɛznt̩ ‖ ðɛə̯r ɪz ə fiːlɪŋ ɪgzæktli laɪ̯k 'ðæt | wʌn həz əpɒn ə 'swɪʧbæk | əv ə 'hɛlpləs hɛdlɒŋ 'məʊ̯ʃn̩ ‖ aɪ̯ fɛlt ðə seɪ̯m hɒrəbl̩ æntɪsɪ'peɪ̯ʃn̩ 'tuː | əv ən ɪmɪnənt 'smæʃ ‖ əz aɪ̯ pʊt ɒn 'peɪ̯s | 'naɪ̯t fɒlə̯ʊ̯d 'deɪ̯ | laɪ̯k ðə 'flæpɪŋ əv ə blæk 'wɪŋ ‖ ðə dɪm sə'ʤɛsʧn̩ əv ðə lə'bɒrətəri | siːmd 'prɛzn̩tli tə fɔːl ə'weɪ̯ frəm miː | ənd aɪ̯ sɔː ðə 'sʌn | hɒpɪŋ 'swɪftli əkrɒs ðə 'skaɪ̯ | 'liːpɪŋ ɪt ɛvri 'mɪnɪt | ənd ɛvri 'mɪnɪt | mɑːkɪŋ ə 'deɪ̯ ‖ aɪ̯ səpəʊ̯zd ðə lə'bɒrətəri | həd biːn dɪ'strɔɪ̯d | ənd aɪ̯ həd 'kʌm ɪntə ði əʊ̯pn̩ 'ɛə̯]

🇺🇸 [aɪ̯ əm ə'freɪ̯d aɪ̯ kænɑːt kən'veɪ̯ | ðə pɪkjuːljɚ sɛn'seɪ̯ʃn̩z əv 'taɪm trævəlɪŋ ‖ ðeɪ̯ ɑːr ɪk'sɛsɪvli ʌn'plɛznt̩ ‖ ðɛr ɪz ə fiːlɪŋ ɪgzæktli laɪ̯k 'ðæt | wʌn həz əpɑːn ə 'swɪʧbæk | əv ə 'hɛlpləs hɛdlɔːŋ 'moʊ̯ʃn̩ ‖ aɪ̯ fɛlt ðə seɪ̯m hɔːrəbl̩ æntɪsɪ'peɪ̯ʃn̩ 'tuː | əv ən ɪmɪnənt 'smæʃ ‖ əz aɪ̯ pʊt ɑːn 'peɪ̯s | 'naɪ̯t fɑːlə̯ʊ̯d 'deɪ̯ | laɪ̯k ðə 'flæpɪŋ əv ə blæk 'wɪŋ ‖ ðə dɪm səg'ʤɛsʧn̩ əv ðə 'læbrətɔːri| siːmd 'prɛzn̩tli tə fɔːl ə'weɪ̯ frəm miː | ənd aɪ̯ sɔː ðə 'sʌn | hɑːpɪŋ 'swɪftli əkrɔːs ðə 'skaɪ̯ | 'liːpɪŋ ɪt ɛvri 'mɪnət | ənd ɛvri 'mɪnət | mɑːrkɪŋ ə 'deɪ̯ ‖ aɪ̯ səpoʊ̯zd ðə 'læbrətɔːri | həd biːn dɪ'strɔɪ̯d | ənd aɪ̯ həd 'kʌm ɪntə ði oʊ̯pn̩ 'ɛr]

3.1

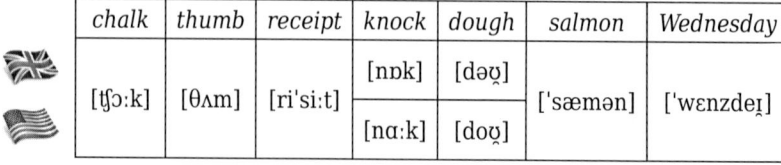

	chalk	thumb	receipt	knock	dough	salmon	Wednesday
	[ʧɔːk]	[θʌm]	[riˈsiːt]	[nɒk]	[dəʊ̯]	[ˈsæmən]	[ˈwɛnzdeɪ̯]
				[nɑːk]	[doʊ̯]		

	debt	calm	honest	wrap	subtle	yacht	mnemonics
	[dɛt]	[kɑːm]	[ˈɒnɪst]	[ræp]	[ˈsʌtəl]	[jɒt]	[nɪˈmɒnɪks]
			[ˈɑːnəst]			[jɑːt]	[nɪˈmɑːnɪks]

	vehicle	gnome	damn	calve	muscle	ghost	handsome
	[ˈviːɪkəl]	[nəʊ̯m]	[dæm]	[kɑːv]	[ˈmʌsəl]	[gəʊ̯st]	[ˈhænsəm]
		[noʊ̯m]		[kæv]		[goʊ̯st]	

	womb	weigh	psycho	isle	solemn	wrist	sovereign
	[wuːm]	[weɪ̯]	[ˈsaɪ̯kəʊ̯]	[aɪ̯l]	[ˈsɒləm]	[rɪst]	[ˈsɒvrɪn]
			[ˈsaɪ̯koʊ̯]		[ˈsɑːləm]		[ˈsɑːvrən]

	doubt	sign	reign	tomb	hour	folk	heir
	[daʊ̯t]	[saɪn]	[reɪ̯n]	[tuːm]	[ˈaʊ̯ə]	[fəʊ̯k]	[ɛə]
					[ˈaʊ̯ɚ]	[foʊ̯k]	[ɛr]

3.2

enough			[f]	
action				[ʃ]
chips		[tʃ]		
occasion				[ʒ]
accent	[ks]			
scheme			[k]	

3.3

Both [m] and [p] are bilabial sounds and the lips are relatively easy to move. Other articulatory movements, such as lifting the tongue backwards, are comparatively harder, so that children learn velar sounds like [k] or [g] much later. When children utter sound sequences that sound like (mama) or (papa), they are often just making first steps in gaining control over their speech organs.

3.4

Gulliver's Travels by Jonathan Swift

[aɪ ə'tɛmptɪd tə 'raɪz | bət wəz nɒt eɪbl̩ tə 'stɜː | fɔː | əz aɪ 'hæpn̩d tə laɪ ɒn maɪ 'bæk | aɪ faʊnd maɪ ɑːmz ənd 'lɛgz | wə strɒŋli 'fɑːsn̩d | ɒn iːtʃ 'saɪd tə ðə 'graʊnd ‖ aɪ hɜːd ə kənfjuːzd 'nɔɪz əbaʊt mi | bət ɪn ðə 'pɒstʃə aɪ 'leɪ | kʊd siː 'nʌθɪŋ ɪksɛpt ðə 'skaɪ ‖ ɪn ə lɪtl̩ 'taɪm | aɪ fɛlt sʌmθɪŋ ə'laɪv | muːvɪŋ ɒn maɪ lɛft 'lɛg | wɪtʃ | ədvɑːnsɪŋ dʒɛntli 'fɔːwəd oʊvə maɪ 'brɛst | keɪm 'ɔːlməʊst ʌp tə maɪ 'tʃɪn | wɛn bɛndɪŋ maɪ aɪz 'daʊnwədz əz mʌtʃ əz aɪ 'kʊd | aɪ pə'siːvd ɪt | tə bi ə hjuːmən 'kriːtʃə | nɒt 'sɪks ɪntʃɪz haɪ | wɪð ə bəʊ ənd 'ærəʊ ɪn hɪz hændz | ənd ə 'kwɪvər ət hɪz 'bæk]

[aɪ ə'tɛmptɪd tə 'raɪz | bət wəz nɑːt eɪbl̩ tə 'stɜ˞ | fɔːr | əz aɪ 'hæpn̩d tə laɪ ɑːn maɪ 'bæk | aɪ faʊnd maɪ ɑːrmz ənd 'lɛgz | wə˞ strɑːŋli 'fæsn̩d | ɑːn iːtʃ 'saɪd tə ðə 'graʊnd ‖ aɪ hɜ˞d ə kənfjuːzd 'nɔɪz əbaʊt mi | bət ɪn ðə 'pɑːstʃə˞ aɪ 'leɪ | kʊd siː 'nʌθɪŋ ɪksɛpt ðə 'skaɪ ‖ ɪn ə lɪtl̩ 'taɪm | aɪ fɛlt sʌmθɪŋ ə'laɪv | muːvɪŋ ɑːn maɪ lɛft 'lɛg | wɪtʃ | ədvænsɪŋ dʒɛntli 'fɔːrwə˞d oʊvə˞ maɪ 'brɛst | keɪm 'ɔːlmoʊst ʌp tə maɪ 'tʃɪn | wɛn bɛndɪŋ maɪ aɪz 'daʊnwə˞dz əz mʌtʃ əz aɪ 'kʊd | aɪ̯ pɚ'siːvd ɪt | tə bi ə hjuːmən 'kriːtʃɚ | nɑːt 'sɪks ɪntʃɪz haɪ̯ | wɪθ ə boʊ̯ ənd 'æroʊ̯ ɪn hɪz hændz | ənd ə 'kwɪvɚ ət hɪz 'bæk]

4.1

		🇬🇧 🇺🇸			🇬🇧 🇺🇸			🇬🇧 🇺🇸
(u)	use	[juːz]	put	[pʊt]	cut	[kʌt]
	burn	[bɜːn] [bɝːn]	cure	[kjʊə̯] [kjʊr]	sure	[ʃɔː] [ʃʊr]
(a)	make	[meɪ̯k]	mad	[mæd]	far	[fɑː] [fɑːr]
	warn	[wɔːn] [wɔːrn]	want	[wɒnt] [wɑːnt]	many	[mɛni]
(o)	code	[kəʊ̯d] [koʊ̯d]	job	[dʒɒb] [dʒɑːb]	short	[ʃɔːt] [ʃɔːrt]
	come	[kʌm]	word	[wɜːd] [wɝːd]	move	[muːv]
(e)	well	[wɛl]	be	[biː]	they	[ðeɪ̯]
	here	[hɪə̯] [hɪr]	there	[ðɛə̯] [ðɛr]	were	[wɜː] [wɝː]
(i)	time	[taɪ̯m]	give	[gɪv]	stir	[stɜː] [stɝː]

4.2

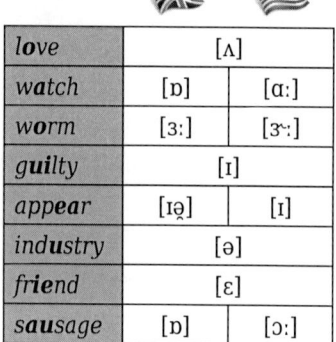

	🇬🇧	🇺🇸
love	[ʌ]	
watch	[ɒ]	[ɑː]
worm	[ɜː]	[ɝː]
guilty	[ɪ]	
appear	[ɪə̯]	[ɪ]
industry	[ə]	
friend	[ɛ]	
sausage	[ɒ]	[ɔː]

4.3

The War of the Worlds by H. G. Wells

[ɑːftə ðə ˈglɪmps aɪ həd hæd əv ðə ˈmɑːʃn̩z | ɪˈmɜːdʒɪŋ frəm ðə ˈsɪlɪndər | ɪn wɪtʃ ðeɪ həd ˈkʌm tə ði ˈɜːθ frəm ðɛə ˈplænɪt | ə kaɪnd əv fæsɪˈneɪʃn̩ | ˈpærəlaɪzd maɪ ˈækʃn̩z ‖ aɪ dɪd nɒt ˈdɛə tə gəʊ ˈbæk təwɔːdz ðə pɪt | bət aɪ fɛlt ə pæʃənət ˈlɒŋɪŋ | tə pɪər ˈɪntu ɪt ‖ aɪ bɪgæn ˈwɔːkɪŋ ðɛəfɔː | ɪn ə bɪg ˈkɜːv | ˈsiːkɪŋ səm pɔɪnt əv ˈvɑːntɪdʒ | ənd kənˈtɪnjuəli ˈlʊkɪŋ ət ðə ˈsænd hiːps | ðət hɪd ðiːz ˈnjuːkʌməz tu aʊər ɜːθ ‖ ˈwʌns | ə ˈliːʃ əv θɪn blæk ˈwɪps | laɪk ði ˈɑːmz əv ən ˈɒktəpəs | ˈflæʃt əkrɒs ðə ˈsʌnsɛt | ənd wəz ɪˈmiːdjətli wɪðˈdrɔːn | ənd ˈɑːftəwədz | ə θɪn ˈrɒd rəʊz ʌp | ˈdʒɔɪnt baɪ ˈdʒɔɪnt | bɛərɪŋ ət ɪts ˈeɪpɛks | ə sɜːkjələ ˈdɪsk | ðət ˈspʌn wɪð ə wɒblɪŋ ˈməʊʃn̩]

[æftɚ ðə ˈglɪmps aɪ həd hæd əv ðə ˈmɑːrʃn̩z | ɪˈmɜˑdʒɪŋ frəm ðə ˈsɪlɪndɚ | ɪn wɪtʃ ðeɪ həd ˈkʌm tə ði ˈɜˑθ frəm ðɛr ˈplænɪt | ə kaɪnd əv fæsɪˈneɪʃn̩ | ˈpærəlaɪzd maɪ ˈækʃn̩z ‖ aɪ dɪd nɑːt ˈdɛr tə goʊ ˈbæk təwɔːrdz ðə pɪt | bət aɪ fɛlt ə pæʃənət ˈlɔːŋɪŋ | tə pɪr ˈɪntu ɪt ‖ aɪ bɪgæn ˈwɔːkɪŋ ðɛrfɔːr | ɪn ə bɪg ˈkɜˑv | ˈsiːkɪŋ səm pɔɪnt əv ˈvæntɪdʒ | ənd kənˈtɪnjuəli ˈlʊkɪŋ ət ðə ˈsænd hiːps | ðət hɪd ðiːz ˈnuːkʌmɚz tu aʊɚ ɜˑθ ‖ ˈwʌns | ə ˈliːʃ əv θɪn blæk ˈwɪps | laɪk ði ˈɑːrmz əv ən ˈɑːktəpəs | ˈflæʃt əkrɑːs ðə ˈsʌnsɛt | ənd wəz ɪˈmiːdjətli wɪðˈdrɔːn | ənd ˈæftɚwɚdz | ə θɪn ˈrɑːd roʊz ʌp | ˈdʒɔɪnt baɪ ˈdʒɔɪnt | bɛrɪŋ ət ɪts ˈeɪpɛks | ə sɜˑkjələ ˈdɪsk | ðət ˈspʌn wɪθ ə wɑːblɪŋ ˈmoʊʃn̩]

5.1

a) James McAvoy
b) Nicole Kidman
c) Hugh Jackman
d) Angelia Jolie

5.2

Pitch measures how often the vocal folds vibrate in a second. Since [s] is a voiceless sound and the vocal folds do not vibrate, there is no pitch.

5.3

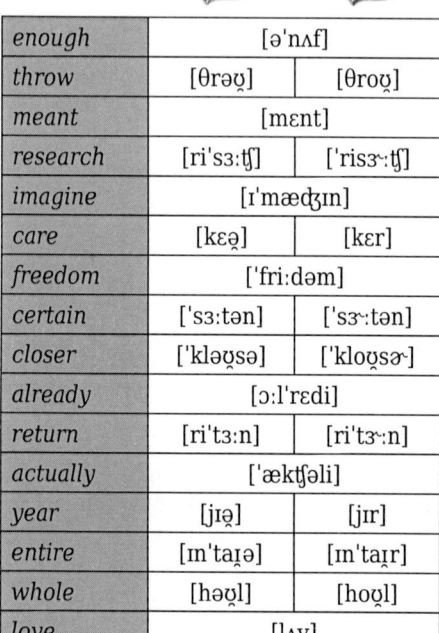

enough	[ə'nʌf]	
throw	[θrəʊ̯]	[θroʊ̯]
meant	[mɛnt]	
research	[ri'sɜ:tʃ]	['risɚ:tʃ]
imagine	[ɪ'mæʤɪn]	
care	[kɛə̯]	[kɛr]
freedom	['fri:dəm]	
certain	['sɜ:tən]	['sɜˑ:tən]
closer	['kləʊ̯sə]	['kloʊ̯sɚ]
already	[ɔ:l'rɛdi]	
return	[ri't3:n]	[ri't3ˑ:n]
actually	['æktʃəli]	
year	[jɪə̯]	[jɪr]
entire	[ɪn'taɪ̯ə]	[ɪn'taɪ̯r]
whole	[həʊ̯l]	[hoʊ̯l]
love	[lʌv]	

5.4

Peter Pan by J. M. Barrie

[fi:lɪŋ | ðət 'pi:tə wəz ɒn hɪz weɪ̯ 'bæk | ðə 'nɛvəlænd | həd əgɛn wəʊ̯k ɪntə 'laɪ̯f ‖ wi ɔ:t tə ju:z ðə 'plu:pɜ:fɪkt | ənd seɪ̯ 'weɪ̯kənd | bət wəʊ̯k ɪz 'bɛtər | ənd wəz ɔ:lweɪ̯z ju:zd baɪ̯ 'pi:tə ‖ ɪn hɪz 'æbsəns | θɪŋz ɑ: ju:ʒəli 'kwaɪ̯ət ɒn ði aɪ̯lənd ‖ ðə 'fɛə̯riz | teɪ̯k ən aʊ̯ə 'lɒŋgər ɪn ðə mɔ:nɪŋ | ðə 'bi:sts | ətɛnd tə ðɛə̯ 'jʌŋ | ðə 'rɛdskɪnz | fi:d 'hɛvɪli fə sɪks deɪ̯z ənd 'naɪ̯ts | ənd wɛn 'paɪ̯rəts ənd lɒst bɔɪ̯z 'mi:t | ðeɪ̯ mɪə̯li baɪ̯t ðɛə̯ 'θʌmz ət i:tʃ ʌðə | bət wɪð ðə kʌmɪŋ əv 'pi:tə | hu 'heɪ̯ts lɛθəʤi | ðeɪ̯ ɑ:r ʌndə 'weɪ̯ əgɛn | ɪf ju pʊt jɔ:r 'ɪə̯ tə ðə 'graʊ̯nd naʊ̯ | ju wʊd hɪə̯ ðə həʊ̯l 'aɪ̯lənd | si:ðɪŋ wɪð 'laɪ̯f]

[fi:lɪŋ | ðət 'pi:tɚ wəz ɑ:n hɪz weɪ̯ 'bæk | ðə 'nɛvɚlænd | həd əgɛn woʊ̯k ɪntə 'laɪ̯f ‖ wi ɔ:t tə ju:z ðə 'plu:pɜ:fɪkt | ənd seɪ̯ 'weɪ̯kənd | bət woʊ̯k ɪz 'bɛtɚ | ənd wəz ɔ:lweɪ̯z ju:zd baɪ̯ 'pi:tɚ ‖ ɪn hɪz 'æbsəns | θɪŋz ɑ:r ju:ʒəli 'kwaɪ̯ət ɑ:n ði aɪlənd ‖ ðə 'fɛriz | teɪk ən aʊ̯ə˞ 'lɔːŋgə˞ ɪn ðə mɔːrnɪŋ | ðə 'biːsts | ətɛnd tə ðɛr 'jʌŋ | ðə 'rɛdskɪnz | fiːd 'hɛvɪli fə˞ sɪks deɪz ənd 'naɪts | ənd wɛn 'paɪrəts ənd lɔːst bɔɪz 'miːt | ðeɪ mɪrli baɪt ðɛr 'θʌmz ət iːtʃ ʌðə˞ | bət wɪθ ðə kʌmɪŋ əv 'piːtə˞ | hu 'heɪts lɛθə˞dʒi | ðeɪ ɑːr ʌndə˞ 'weɪ əgɛn | ɪf ju pʊt jʊr 'ɪr tə ðə 'graʊnd naʊ̯ | ju wʊd hɪr ðə hoʊ̯l 'aɪlənd | siːðɪŋ wɪθ 'laɪf]

6.1

/d/	alveolar [d]	*drag*	post-alveolar [ɖ]
/n/	alveolar [n]	*labyrinth*	dental [n̪]
/m/	bilabial [m]	*symphony*	labiodental [ɱ]
/t/	alveolar [t]	*tool*	alveolar, labialised [tʷ]
/k/	velar [k]	*keep*	pre-velar [k̟]

6.2

perfect	['pɜːfɪkt]	['pɝːfɪkt]
collect	[kə'lɛkt]	
suppose	[sə'pəʊ̯z]	[sə'poʊ̯z]
country	['kʌntri]	
project	['prɒdʒɛkt]	['prɑːdʒɛkt]
journey	['dʒɜːni]	['dʒɝːni]
action	['ækʃn̩]	
occur	[ə'kɜː]	[ə'kɝː]
money	['mʌni]	
gesture	['dʒɛstʃə]	['dʒɛstʃə˞]
injure	['ɪndʒə]	['ɪndʒə˞]
language	['læŋgwɪdʒ]	
stranger	['streɪndʒə]	['streɪndʒə˞]
stove	[stəʊ̯v]	[stoʊ̯v]
examine	[ɪg'zæmɪn]	
somebody	['sʌmbədi]	

6.3

Journey to the Centre of the Earth by Jules Vernes
(narrow transcription)

[ðə 'kʰəʊ̯ɫd ɪn ðə ʃeɪ̯dz əv ðɪs sɪŋgjʊlə 'fʊɹɪst | wəz ɪn'tʰɛns ‖ fə nɪə̯li ən 'aʊ̯ə | wi wɒndəd ə'baʊ̯t ɪn ðɪs vɪzəbɫ̩ 'dɑːknəs ‖ ət̚ 'lɛŋθ | aɪ̯ lɛft ðə 'spɒtʰ | ənd wʌns mʷɔː ɹɪ'tʰɜːnd̚ | tə ðə 'ʃʷɔːz əv ðə leɪ̯kʰ | tə 'laɪ̯t ən̩d kəmpʰæɹətʰɪv 'wɔːmθ ‖ bət ði əmeɪ̯zɪŋ vɛʤə'tʰeɪ̯ʃn̩ əɣ sʌb̥ʰəɹeɪ̯niəs 'lænd | wəz nɒt kʰən'faɪ̯n̩d̚ tə ʤaɪ̯gæntʰɪk 'mʌʃɹʊmz ‖ nju: 'wʌndəz | əweɪ̯tʰɪd ʌz ət ɛvɹi 'stɛpʰ ‖ wi həd nɒt gɒn mɛni hʌndɹəd 'jɑːʤ | wɛn wi kʰeɪ̯m əpʰɒn ə maɪ̯tʰi 'gɹʷuːpʰ əv 'ʌðə t̪ʰɹiːz | wɪð dɪskʰʌɫəd 'liːvz̩]

[ðə 'kʰoʊ̯ɫd ɪn ðə ʃeɪ̯dz əv ðɪs sɪŋgjəɫɚ 'fɔːɹəst | wəz ɪn'tʰɛns ‖ fɚ nɪɹɫi ən 'aʊ̯ɚ | wi wɑːndɚd ə'baʊ̯t ɪn ðɪs vɪzəbɫ̩ 'dɑːɹknəs ‖ ət̚ 'lɛŋθ | aɪ̯ lɛft ðə 'spɑːtʰ | ənd wʌns mʷɔːɹ ɹɪ'tʰɜ̊ːnd̚ |tə ðə 'ʃʷɔːɹz əv ðə ɫeɪ̯kʰ | tə 'laɪ̯t ən̩d kəmpʰæɹətɪv 'wɔːɹmθ ‖ bət ði əmeɪ̯zɪŋ vɛʤə'tʰeɪ̯ʃn̩ əɣ sʌb̥ʰəɹeɪ̯niəs 'ɫænd | wəz nɑːt kʰən'faɪ̯n̩d̚ tə ʤaɪ̯gæntɪk 'mʌʃɹuːmz ‖ nu: 'wʌndɚz | əweɪ̯t̬ɪd ʌz ət ɛvɹi 'stɛpʰ ‖ wi həd nɑːt gɔːn mɛni hʌndɹəd 'jɑːɹdʒ | wɛn wi kʰeɪ̯m əpʰɑːn ə maɪ̯t̬i 'gɹʷuːpʰ əv 'ʌðɚ t̪ʰɹiːz | wɪθ d̬ɪskʰʌɫɚd 'ɫiːvz̩]

6.4

Les Misérables by Victor Hugo

When Fantine saw that she was making her living, she felt joyful for a moment. To live honestly by her own labor, what mercy from heaven! The taste for work had really returned to her. She bought a looking-glass, took pleasure in surveying in it her youth, her beautiful hair, her fine teeth; she forgot many things.

7.1

job	[dʒɒb]
bank	[bæŋk]
stronger	[ˈstrɒŋgə]
sight	[sa̝ɪt]
cutter	[ˈkʌtə]
company	[ˈkʌmpəni]
uninvited	[ʌnɪnˈva̝ɪtɪd]

7.2

a)

[pɪn]	[bɪn]	[tɪn]	[dɪn]	[kɪn]	[t͡ʃɪn]	[d͡ʒɪn]
pin	bin	tin	din	kin	chin	gin

[fɪn]	[θɪn]	[sɪn]	[ʃɪn]	[wɪn]	[jɪn]	[mɪn]
fin	thin	sin	shin	win	yin	min.

b)

[hiːd]	[hɪd]	[hɛd]	[hæd]	[hʊd]	[huːd]	[ha̯ʊd]
heed	hid	head	had	hood	who'd	how'd

[ha̝ɪd]	[həʊ̯d]	[hɜːd]	[hɛə̯d]	[hɑːd]	[hɒd]	[hɔːd]
	[hoʊ̯d]	[hɝːd]	—	—	[hɑːd]	—
hide	hoed	heard	haired	hard	hod	hoard

c)

[rɪp]	[rɪb]	[rɪd]	[rɪt]	[rɪk]	[rɪg]
rip	rib	rid	writ	rick	rig

[rɪt͡ʃ]	[rɪd͡ʒ]	[rɪf]	[rɪm]	[rɪŋ]	[rɪl]
rich	ridge	riff	rim	ring	rill

7.3

trap		palm		bath	🇬🇧	🇺🇸
crash	[kræʃ]	father	['fɑːðə]/[ɚ]	last	[lɑːst]	[læst]
math	[mæθ]	calm	[kɑːm]	after	['ɑːftə]	['æftɚ]
random	['rændm̩]	almond	['ɑːmənd]	glass	[glɑːs]	[glæs]
tap	[tæp]	drama	['drɑːmə]	laughter	['lɑːftə]	['læftɚ]
ham	[hæm]	bra	[brɑː]	ask	[ɑːsk]	[æsk]
sack	[sæk]			rather	['rɑːðə]	['ræðɚ]
arrow	['ærəʊ]/[oʊ]			chance	[ʧɑːns]	[ʧæns]
mass	[mæs]			demand	[diˈmɑːnd]	[diˈmænd]

7.4

The Fall of the House of Usher by Edgar Allan Poe
(narrow transcription)

🇬🇧 [djʊə̯ɹɪŋ ðə həʊ̯ł əv ə 'dʌł 'dɑːk ənd 'saʊ̯ndləs 'deɪ̯ | ɪn ði 'ɔːtʰm̩ əv ðə 'jɪə̯ɹ | wɛn ðə 'kʰłaʊ̯dz̥ hʌŋ əpʰɹɛsɪvli 'ləʊ̯ ɪn ðə hɛvn̩z̥ | aɪ̯ həd biːn 'pʰɑːsɪŋ ə'ləʊ̯n | ɒn 'hʷɔːsbæk | θ.ɹʷuː ə sɪŋgjʊləli 'dɹɪə̯.ɹi tʰ.ɹækt əɣ 'kʰʌntʰ.ɹi | ənd ətʰˌlɛŋθ 'faʊ̯nd maɪ̯sɛłf | əz ðə 'ʃeɪ̯dz əv ði 'iːvnɪŋ d.ɹʷuː ɒn | wɪðɪn 'vjuː əv ðə 'mɛlənkʰəli haʊ̯s əv 'ʌʃə || aɪ̯ 'nəʊ̯ nɒt haʊ̯ ɪt 'wɒz̥ | bʌtʰ | wɪð ðə fɜːst 'glɪmps əv ðə bɪłdɪŋ | ə sɛns əv ɪnsʌfɹəbl̩ 'głʷuːm | pʰəveɪ̯dɪd maɪ̯ 'spɪɹɪtʰ]

🇺🇸 [djɜˑɪŋ ðə hoʊ̯ł əv ə 'dʌł 'dɑːɹk ənd 'saʊ̯ndłəs 'deɪ̯ | ɪn ði 'ɔːtm̩ əv ðə 'jɪɹ | wɛn ðə 'kʰłaʊ̯dz̥ hʌŋ əpʰɹɛsɪvłi 'łoʊ̯ ɪn ðə hɛvn̩z̥ | aɪ̯ həd biːn 'pʰæsɪŋ ə'łoʊ̯n | ɑːn 'hʷɔːɹsbæk | θ.ɹʷuː ə sɪŋgjəłɚłi 'dɹɪɹi tʰ.ɹækt əɣ 'kʰʌntʰ.ɹi | ənd ətʰˌlɛŋθ 'faʊ̯nd maɪ̯sɛłf | əz ðə 'ʃeɪ̯dz əv ði 'iːvnɪŋ d.ɹʷuː ɑːn | wɪðɪn 'vjuː əv ðə 'mɛlənkʰɑːłi haʊ̯s əv 'ʌʃɚ || aɪ̯ 'noʊ̯ nɑːt haʊ̯ ɪt 'wʌz̥ | bʌtʰ | wɪθ ðə fɜˑɹst 'glɪmps əv ðə bɪłdɪŋ | ə sɛns əv ɪnsʌfɹəbl̩ 'głʷuːm | pʰɚveɪ̯dɪd maɪ̯ 'spɪɹətʰ]

7.5

Jane Eyre by Charlotte Brontë

It was very near, but not yet in sight; when, in addition to the tramp, tramp, I heard a rush under the hedge, and close down by the hazel stems glided a great dog, whose black and white colour made him a distinct object against the trees. The dog came bounding back, and seeing his master in a predicament, and hearing the horse groan, barked till the evening hills echoed the sound, which was deep in proportion to his magnitude.

8.1

1) Antarctic
2) France is near
3) matador
4) anonymous
5) ice cream
6) I leaned over
7) microbe
8) gate open
9) glad he's back
10) robbin' banks
11) just in case it burns
12) I rode a camel
13) you go first
14) burn a debt collector
15) antelope

8.2

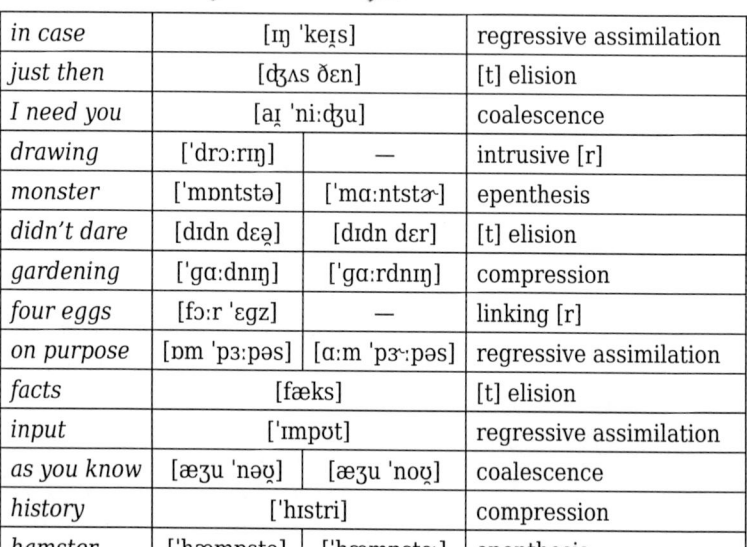

in case	[ɪŋ ˈkeɪ̯s]		regressive assimilation
just then	[dʒʌs ðɛn]		[t] elision
I need you	[aɪ̯ ˈniːdʒu]		coalescence
drawing	[ˈdrɔːrɪŋ]	—	intrusive [r]
monster	[ˈmɒntstə]	[ˈmɑːntstɚ]	epenthesis
didn't dare	[dɪdn dɛə̯]	[dɪdn dɛr]	[t] elision
gardening	[ˈgɑːdnɪŋ]	[ˈgɑːrdnɪŋ]	compression
four eggs	[fɔːr ˈɛgz]	—	linking [r]
on purpose	[ɒm ˈpɜːpəs]	[ɑːm ˈpɝːpəs]	regressive assimilation
facts	[fæks]		[t] elision
input	[ˈɪmpʊt]		regressive assimilation
as you know	[æʒu ˈnəʊ̯]	[æʒu ˈnoʊ̯]	coalescence
history	[ˈhɪstri]		compression
hamster	[ˈhæmpstə]	[ˈhæmpstɚ]	epenthesis
bacon	[ˈbeɪ̯kn̩]		progressive assimilation

8.3

The Wonderful Wizard of Oz by L. Frank Baum

[ɑːftər ə fjuː ˈaʊ̯əz | ðə ˈrəʊ̯d bɪgæn tə bi ˈrʌf | ənd ðə ˈwɔːkɪŋ | gruː səʊ̯ ˈdɪfɪkəlt ðət ðə ˈskɛə̯krəʊ̯ | ɒfn̩ ˈstʌmbl̩d əʊ̯və ðə jɛləʊ̯ ˈbrɪks | wɪtʃ wə ˈhɪə̯ vɛri ʌnˈiːvn̩ ‖ sʌmtaɪ̯mz ɪnˈdiːd | ðeɪ̯ wə ˈbrəʊ̯kən | ɔː mɪsɪŋ ɔːltəˈgɛðə | liːvɪŋ ˈhəʊ̯lz ðət təʊ̯təʊ̯ dʒʌmpt əˈkrɒs | ənd ˈdɒrəθi wɔːkt əˈraʊ̯nd ‖ əz fə ðə ˈskɛə̯krəʊ̯ | hævɪŋ nəʊ̯ ˈbreɪ̯nz | hi wɔːkt streɪ̯t əˈhɛd | ənd səʊ̯ stɛpt ˈɪntuː ðə həʊ̯lz | ənd fɛl ət fʊl ˈlɛŋkθ | ɒn ðə hɑːd ˈbrɪks ‖ ɪt nɛvə ˈhɜːt hɪm haʊ̯ɛvə | ənd ˈdɒrəθi wʊd pɪk hɪm ˈʌp | ənd ˈsɛt hɪm əpɒn hɪz ˈfiːt əgɛn | waɪ̯l hi ˈdʒɔɪ̯nd hər ɪn lɑːfɪŋ ˈmɛrɪli | ət hɪz əʊ̯n ˈmɪshæp]

[æftɚ ə fjuː ˈaʊ̯ɚz | ðə ˈroʊ̯d bɪgæn tə bi ˈrʌf | ənd ðə ˈwɔːkɪŋ | gruː soʊ̯ ˈdɪfɪkəlt ðət ðə ˈskɛrkroʊ̯ | ɔːfn̩ ˈstʌmbl̩d oʊ̯vɚ ðə jɛloʊ̯ ˈbrɪks | wɪtʃ wɚ ˈhɪr vɛri ʌnˈiːvn̩ ‖ sʌmtaɪ̯mz ɪnˈdiːd | ðeɪ̯ wɚ ˈbroʊ̯kən | ɔːr mɪsɪŋ ɔːltəˈgɛðɚ | liːvɪŋ ˈhoʊ̯lz ðət toʊ̯toʊ̯ dʒʌmpt əˈkrɔːs | ənd ˈdɔːrəθi wɔːkt əˈraʊ̯nd ‖ əz fɚ ðə ˈskɛrkroʊ̯ |

hævɪŋ noṷ ˈbreɪ̯nz | hi wɔːkt streɪ̯t əˈhɛd | ənd soṷ stɛpt ˈɪntuː ðə hoṷlz | ənd fɛl ət fʊl ˈlɛŋkθ | ɑːn ðə hɑːrd ˈbrɪks ‖ ɪt nɛvɚ ˈhɝːt hɪm haṷɛvɚ | ənd ˈdɔːrəθi wʊd pɪk hɪm ˈʌp | ənd ˈsɛt hɪm əpɑːn hɪz ˈfiːt əgɛn | waɪ̯l hi ˈʤɔɪ̯nd hɚ ɪn læfɪŋ ˈmɛrɪli | ət hɪz oṷn ˈmɪshæp]

8.4

A Study in Scarlet by Sir Arthur Conan Doyle

This was a lofty chamber, lined and littered with countless bottles. Broad, low tables were scattered about, which bristled with retorts, test-tubes, and little Bunsen lamps, with their blue flickering flames. There was only one student in the room, who was bending over a distant table absorbed in his work. At the sound of our steps he glanced round and sprang to his feet with a cry of pleasure.

9.1

a)

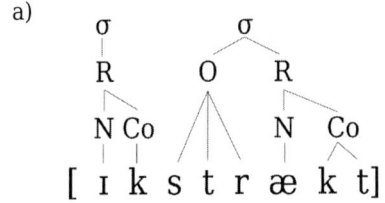

maximum onset: [ɪ.ˈkstrækt]
onset constraints: [ɪk.ˈstrækt]

b)

maximum onset: [ˈʤʌ.ŋktʃə]
onset constraints: [ˈʤʌŋk.tʃə]

c)

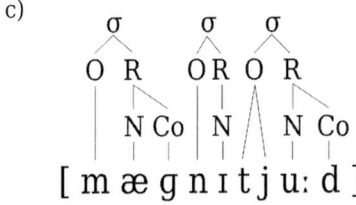

maximum onset: [ˈmæ.gnɪ.tjuːd]
onset constraints: [ˈmæg.nɪ.tjuːd]

d)

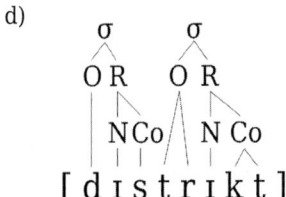

maximum onset: [ˈdɪ.strɪkt]
stressed checked vowel: [ˈdɪs.trɪkt]

9.2

[freɪ̞h]	[h] cannot occur in a coda
[ʃvɛk]	[ʃv] is not an admissible onset cluster
[ʒɪlf]	[ʒ] cannot occur in an onset
[sprʊŋk]	admissible word
[knəʊ̞]	[kn] is not an admissible onset cluster
[skwɒltʃ]	admissible word

9.3

Which consonants are allowed in the onset or coda of a syllable, differs from language to language (phonotactic constraints). As Japanase hardly allows consonants in the coda of a syllable, additional vowels are inserted.

9.4

Dracula by Bram Stoker

[ðɛn wɪð 'swɪftnəs | bət wɪð æbsəlu:t 'mɛθəd | væn 'hɛlsɪŋ pəfɔːmd ði ɒpə'reɪʃn̩ ‖ əz ðə træns'fjuːʒn̩ wɛnt 'ɒn | sʌmθɪŋ laɪ̞k 'laɪ̞f | siːmd tə kʌm 'bæk tə pʊə̞ luːsiz 'tʃiːks | ənd θruː 'ɑːθəz grəʊ̞ɪŋ 'pælə | ðə dʒɔɪ̞ əv hɪz 'feɪ̞s | siːmd æbsəluːtli tə 'ʃaɪ̞n ‖ ɑːftər ə 'bɪt | aɪ̞ bɪgæn tə grəʊ̞ 'æŋkʃəs | fɔː ðə lɒs əv 'blʌd | wəz tɛlɪŋ ɒn 'ɑːθə | strɒŋ 'mæn əz hi 'wɒz | ɪt geɪ̞v mi ən aɪ̞'dɪə̞ | əv wɒt ə tɛrəbl̩ 'streɪ̞n luːsiz 'sɪstəm mʌst əv ʌndəgɒn | ðət wɒt wiːkənd 'ɑːθə | əʊ̞nli 'pɑːʃəli rɪstɔːd 'hɜː]

[ðɛn wɪθ 'swɪftnəs | bət wɪθ æbsəluːt 'mɛθəd | væn 'hɛlsɪŋ pɚfɔːrmd ði ɑːpə'reɪʃn̩ ‖ əz ðə træns'fjuːʒn̩ wɛnt 'ɑːn | sʌmθɪŋ laɪ̞k 'laɪ̞f | siːmd tə kʌm 'bæk tə pʊr luːsiz 'tʃiːks | ənd θruː 'ɑːrðɚz grouɪ̞ŋ 'pælɚ | ðə dʒɔɪ̞ əv hɪz 'feɪ̞s | siːmd æbsəluːtli tə 'ʃaɪ̞n ‖ æftɚ ə 'bɪt | aɪ̞ bɪgæn tə grou 'æŋkʃəs | fɔːr ðə lɔːs əv 'blʌd | wəz tɛlɪŋ ɑːn 'ɑːrðɚ | strɔːŋ 'mæn əz hi 'wʌz | ɪt geɪ̞v mi ən aɪ̞'dɪr | əv wʌt ə tɛrəbl̩ 'streɪ̞n luːsiz 'sɪstəm mʌst əv ʌndɚgɔːn | ðət wʌt wiːkənd 'ɑːrðɚ | ounli 'pɑːrʃəli rɪstɔːrd 'hɜ˞ː]

9.5

The Island of Doctor Moreau by H. G. Wells

So I lay still there, until I began to think of food and drink; and at that thought the real hopelessness of my position came home to me. I knew no way of getting anything to eat. I was too ignorant of botany to discover any resort of root or fruit that might lie about me; I had no means of trapping the few rabbits upon the island. It grew blanker the more I turned the prospect over. At last in the desperation of my position, my mind turned to the animal men I had encountered. I tried to find some hope in what I remembered of them.

10.1

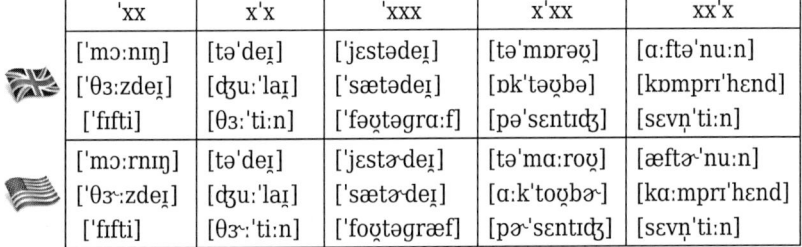

	'xx	x'x	'xxx	x'xx	xx'x
🇬🇧	['mɔːnɪŋ]	[təˈdeɪ]	[ˈjɛstədeɪ]	[təˈmɒrəʊ]	[ɑːftəˈnuːn]
	[ˈθɜːzdeɪ]	[dʒuːˈlaɪ]	[ˈsætədeɪ]	[ɒkˈtəʊbə]	[kɒmprɪˈhɛnd]
	[ˈfɪfti]	[θɜːˈtiːn]	[ˈfəʊtəgrɑːf]	[pəˈsɛntɪdʒ]	[sɛvnˈtiːn]
🇺🇸	['mɔːrnɪŋ]	[təˈdeɪ]	[ˈjɛstɚdeɪ]	[təˈmɑːroʊ]	[æftɚˈnuːn]
	[ˈθɝːzdeɪ]	[dʒuːˈlaɪ]	[ˈsætɚdeɪ]	[ɑːkˈtoʊbɚ]	[kɑːmprɪˈhɛnd]
	[ˈfɪfti]	[θɝːˈtiːn]	[ˈfoʊtəgræf]	[pɚˈsɛntɪdʒ]	[sɛvnˈtiːn]

10.3

Heart of Darkness by Joseph Conrad

🇬🇧 [ə slaɪt ˈklɪŋkɪŋ bɪhaɪnd miː | meɪd mi tɜːn maɪ ˈhɛd ‖ sɪks blæk ˈmɛn ədvɑːnst m ə ˈfaɪl | tɔɪlɪŋ ʌp ðə ˈpɑːθ ‖ ðeɪ wɔːkt ɪˈrɛkt ənd ˈsləʊ | bælənsɪŋ smɔːl ˈbɑːskɪts | fʊl əv ˈɜːθ ɒn ðɛə hɛdz | ənd ðə ˈklɪŋk | kɛpt taɪm wɪð ðɛə ˈfʊtstɛps ‖ blæk ˈrægz | wə waʊnd raʊnd ðɛə ˈlɔɪnz | ənd ðə ʃɔːt ɛndz bɪˈhaɪnd | wægd ˈtuː ənd ˈfrəʊ laɪk teɪlz ‖ aɪ kʊd siː ɛvri ˈrɪb | ðə dʒɔɪnts əv ðɛə ˈlɪmz | wə laɪk nɒts m ə ˈrəʊp | iːʧ həd ən aɪən ˈkɒlər ɒn hɪz nɛk | ənd ɔːl wə kənɛktɪd təˈgɛðə wɪð ə ˈʧeɪn | huːz ˈbaɪts swʌŋ bɪˈtwiːn ðəm | rɪðmɪkli ˈklɪŋkɪŋ]

🇺🇸 [ə slaɪt ˈklɪŋkɪŋ bɪhaɪnd miː | meɪd mi tɝːn maɪ ˈhɛd ‖ sɪks blæk ˈmɛn ədvænst m ə ˈfaɪl | tɔɪlɪŋ ʌp ðə ˈpæθ ‖ ðeɪ wɔːkt ɪˈrɛkt ənd ˈsloʊ | bælənsɪŋ smɔːl ˈbæskəts | fʊl əv ˈɝːθ ɑːn ðɛr hɛdz | ənd ðə ˈklɪŋk | kɛpt taɪm wɪθ ðɛr ˈfʊtstɛps ‖ blæk ˈrægz | wɚ waʊnd raʊnd ðɛr ˈlɔɪnz | ənd ðə ʃɔːrt ɛndz bɪˈhaɪnd

| wægd 'tu: ənd 'froʊ̯ laɪ̯k teɪ̯lz ‖ aɪ̯ kʊd si: ɛvri 'rɪb | ðə ʤɔɪ̯nts əv ðɛr 'lɪmz | wɚ laɪ̯k nɑːts m ə 'roʊ̯p | iːʧ həd ən aɪ̯ɚn 'kɑːlɚ ɑːn hɪz nɛk | ənd ɔːl wɚ kənɛktɪd tə'gɛðɚ wɪθ ə 'ʧeɪ̯n | huːz 'baɪ̯ts swʌŋ bɪ'twiːn ðəm | rɪðmɪkli 'klɪŋkɪŋ]

10.4

The Picture of Dorian Gray by Oscar Wilde

As he was turning the handle of the door, his eye fell upon the portrait Basil Hallward had painted of him. He started back as if in surprise. In the dim arrested light that struggled through the cream-coloured silk blinds, the face appeared to him to be a little changed. The expression looked different. One would have said that there was a touch of cruelty in the mouth. It was certainly strange.

11.1

RP

a) [wɛn aɪ̯ keɪm 'həʊ̯m | ðə tiː'viː wəz stɪl 'rʌnɪŋ]
b) [nəʊ̯ 'stjuːdn̩t mʌst liːv ðə 'ruːm]
c) [pʊt ɪt ɒn ðə 'teɪ̯bl̩ əʊ̯və ðɛə̯]
d) [aɪ̯ 'dəʊ̯nt θɪŋk aɪ̯ 'kæn]
e) [aɪ̯m 'fræŋk | ənd wɒts 'jɔː neɪ̯m]
f) [ʃʊd wi baɪ̯ ðə 'njuː wʌn]

GA

a) [wɛn aɪ̯ keɪm 'hoʊ̯m | ðə tiː'viː wəz stɪl 'rʌnɪŋ]
b) [noʊ̯ 'stuːdn̩t mʌst liːv ðə 'ruːm]
c) [pʊt ɪt ɑːn ðə 'teɪ̯bl̩ oʊ̯vɚ ðɛr]
d) [aɪ̯ 'doʊ̯nt θɪŋk aɪ̯ 'kæn]
e) [aɪ̯m 'fræŋk | ənd wʌts 'jʊr neɪ̯m]
f) [ʃʊd wi baɪ̯ ðə 'nuː wʌn]

11.2

The Strange Case of Dr. Jekyll and Mr. Hyde by Robert Louis Stevenson

🇬🇧 [hi pʊt ðə ˈglɑːs tə hɪz ˈlɪps | ənd dræŋk ət wʌn ˈgʌlp ‖ ə ˈkraɪ fʊləʊd | hi ˈriːld | ˈstæɡəd | klʌʧt ət ðə ˈteɪbl̩ ənd hɛld ˈɒn | ˈsteərɪŋ wɪð ɪnʤɛktɪd ˈaɪz | ˈgɑːspɪŋ wɪð əʊpn̩ ˈmaʊθ | ənd əz aɪ ˈlʊkt | ðɛə ˈkeɪm | aɪ ˈθɔːt | ə ˈʧeɪnʤ | hi siːmd tə ˈswɛl | hɪz feɪs bɪkeɪm sʌdn̩li ˈblæk | ənd ðə ˈfiːʧəz | siːmd tə mɛlt ənd ˈɔːltə | ənd ðə nɛkst ˈməʊmənt | aɪ həd sprʌŋ tə maɪ ˈfiːt | ənd lɛpt ˈbæk əgɛnst ðə ˈwɔːl | maɪ ɑːm ˈreɪzd | tə ʃiːld mi frəm ðæt ˈprɒdəʤi | maɪ ˈmaɪnd | səbmɜːʤd ɪn ˈtɛrə]

🇺🇸 [hi pʊt ðə ˈglæs tə hɪz ˈlɪps | ənd dræŋk ət wʌn ˈgʌlp ‖ ə ˈkraɪ fɑːloʊd | hi ˈriːld | ˈstæɡɚd | klʌʧt ət ðə ˈteɪbl̩ ənd hɛld ˈɑːn | ˈsterɪŋ wɪθ ɪnʤɛktɪd ˈaɪz | ˈgæspɪŋ wɪθ oʊpn̩ ˈmaʊθ | ənd əz aɪ ˈlʊkt | ðɛr ˈkeɪm | aɪ ˈθɔːt | ə ˈʧeɪnʤ | hi siːmd tə ˈswɛl | hɪz feɪs bɪkeɪm sʌdn̩li ˈblæk | ənd ðə ˈfiːʧɚz | siːmd tə mɛlt ənd ˈɔːltɚ | ənd ðə nɛkst ˈmoʊmənt | aɪ həd sprʌŋ tə maɪ ˈfiːt | ənd liːpt ˈbæk əgɛnst ðə ˈwɔːl | maɪ ɑːrm ˈreɪzd | tə ʃiːld mi frəm ðæt ˈprɑːdəʤi | maɪ ˈmaɪnd | səbmɜːˈʤd ɪn ˈtɛrɚ]

11.3

Dubliners by James Joyce

Few people passed. The man out of the last house passed on his way home; she heard his footsteps clacking along the concrete pavement and afterwards crunching on the cinder path before the new red houses. One time there used to be a field there in which they used to play every evening with other people's children. Then a man from Belfast bought the field and built houses in it - not like their little brown houses but bright brick houses with shining roofs.

12.1

a) [wɛə̯ dʊ ju 'θɪŋk jɔː \gəʊ̯ɪŋ]
b) [ɑːftə hi ˅lɛft | ðə 'ruːm wəz mʌtʃ \kwaɪ̯ətə]

c) [sʌtʃ ə \bjuːtəfəl dɒg]
RP
d) [ɑː ju /kʌmɪŋ]
e) [ɑː ju ˅kʌmɪŋ | ɔː \gəʊ̯ɪŋ]
f) [kʌm /ɪn | ənd liːv jɔː \ʃuːz ɒn]

a) [wɛr dʊ ju 'θɪŋk jʊr \goʊ̯ɪŋ]
b) [æftɚ hi ˅lɛft | ðə 'ruːm wəz mʌtʃ \kwaɪ̯ətɚ]

c) [sʌtʃ ə \bjuːtəfəl dɔːg]
GA
d) [ɑːr ju /kʌmɪŋ]
e) [ɑːr ju ˅kʌmɪŋ | ɔːr \goʊ̯ɪŋ]
f) [kʌm /ɪn | ənd liːv jʊr \ʃuːz ɑːn]

12.2

a) tonality (two vs. one intonation phrases)
b) tonicity (stress on ⟨May⟩ vs. ⟨twenty-five⟩)
c) tone (falling vs. rising tone)
d) tone (rising vs. falling tone)
e) tonicity (stress on ⟨thought⟩ vs. ⟨eat⟩)
f) tonality (one vs. two intonation phrases)

12.3

Through the Looking-Glass by Lewis Carroll

[haʊ̯'ɛvə | ði 'ɛg | əʊ̯nli gɒt lɑːdʒər ənd 'lɑːdʒə | ənd mɔːr ənd mɔː 'hjuːmən ‖ wɛn ʃi həd kʌm wɪðɪn ə fjuː 'jɑːdz əv ɪt | ʃi 'sɔː | ðət ɪt həd 'aɪz | ənd ə nəʊ̯z ənd 'maʊ̯θ ‖ ənd wɛn ʃi həd kʌm 'kləʊ̯s tu ɪt | ʃi sɔː 'klɪə̯li | ðət ɪt wəz hʌmpti dʌmpti 'hɪmsɛlf ‖ hʌmpti 'dʌmpti | wəz sɪtɪŋ wɪð hɪz lɛgz 'krɒst | laɪk ə 'tɜːk | ɒn ðə 'tɒp əv ə haɪ̯ 'wɔːl | sʌtʃ ə 'nærəʊ̯ wʌn | ðət ælɪs kwaɪt 'wʌndəd | haʊ̯ hi kʊd kiːp hɪz 'bæləns | ænd əz hɪz aɪ̯z wə stɛdɪli 'fɪkst ɪn ði ɒpəzɪt daɪ̯'rɛkʃn̩ | ənd hi dɪdnt teɪ̯k ðə liːst 'nəʊ̯tɪs əv hɜː | ʃi 'θɔːt | hi mʌst biː ə stʌft fɪgər 'ɑːftər ɔːl]

[haʊ'ɛvɚ | ði 'ɛg | oʊnli gɑːt lɑːrʤɚ ənd 'lɑːrʤɚ | ənd mɔːr ənd mɔːr 'hjuːmən ‖ wɛn ʃi həd kʌm wɪðɪn ə fjuː 'jɑːrdz əv ɪt | ʃi 'sɔː | ðət ɪt həd 'aɪz | ənd ə noʊz ənd 'maʊθ ‖ ənd wɛn ʃi həd kʌm 'kloʊs tu ɪt | ʃi sɔː 'klɪrli | ðət ɪt wəz hʌmpti dʌmpti 'hɪmsɛlf ‖ hʌmpti 'dʌmpti | wəz sɪtɪŋ wɪθ hɪz lɛgz 'krɔːst | laɪk ə 'tɝːk | ɑːn ðə 'tɑːp əv ə haɪ 'wɔːl | sʌʧ ə 'næroʊ wʌn | ðət ælɪs kwaɪt 'wʌndɚd | haʊ hi kʊd kiːp hɪz 'bæləns | ænd əz hɪz aɪz wɚ stɛdɪli 'fɪkst ɪn ði ɑːpəzɪt də'rɛkʃn̩ | ənd hi dɪdnt teɪk ðə liːst 'noʊtɪs əv hɝː | ʃi 'θɔːt | hi mʌst biː ə stʌft fɪgjɚ 'æftɚ ɔːl]

12.4

The Pit and the Pendulum by Edgan Alan Poe

Looking upward, I surveyed the ceiling of my prison. What I then saw confounded and amazed me. The sweep of the pendulum had increased in extent by nearly a yard. As a natural consequence, its velocity was also much greater. But what mainly disturbed me was the idea that it had perceptibly descended. The vibration of the pendulum was at right angles to my length. I saw that the crescent was designed to cross the region of the heart.

Figures and Tables
['fɪɡəz ənd 'teɪbl̩z]

Figures

Tables

Suggested Further Reading
[sə'dʒɛstɪd fɜːðə 'riːdɪŋ]

Pronunciation Dictionaries

Well, John (2008). *Longman Pronunciation Dictionary*. Third edition. Harlow: Pearson Longman.

Roach, Peter et. al (2011). *Cambridge English Pronouncing Dictionary*. 18th edition. Cambridge University Press.

Upton, Clive et. al (2003). *Oxford Dictionary of Pronunciation for Current English*. Oxford University Press.

Books on Phonetics and Phonology

Collins, Beverly and Mees, Inger (2008). *Practical Phonetics and Phonology*. Second edition. London: Routledge

Ashby, Michael and Maidment, John (2008). *Introducing Phonetic Science*. Cambridge University Press.

Wells, John (2006). *English Intonation*. Cambridge University Press.

Cruttenden, Alan (2008). *Gimson's Pronunciation of English*. Seventh edition. London: Hodder Arnold.

Skandera, Paul and Burleigh, Peter (2011). *A Manual of English Phonetics and Phonology*. Second edition. Tübingen: Narr.

Catford, J. C. (2010). *A Practical Introduction to Phonetics*. Second edition. Oxford University Press.

Books on Pronunciation and Transcription

Eckert, Hartwig and Barry, William (2005). *The Phonetics and Phonology of English Pronunciation*. Wissenschaftlicher Verlag Trier.

Tench, Paul (2011). *Transcribing the Sound of English*. Cambridge University Press.

Schmitt, Holger (2011). *Phonetic transcription*. Berlin: Erich-Schmidt-Verlag.

García Lecumberri, María Luisa and Maidment, John (2000). *English Transcription Course*. London: Hodder Arnold.

Pullum, Geoffrey and Ladusaw, William (1996). *Phonetic Symbol Guide*. Second edition. University of Chicago Press.

157

Index of Transcription Texts
['ɪndɛks əv træn'skrɪpʃn̩ tɛksts]

Subject Index

[ˈsʌbdʒɛkt ɪndɛks]

Acknowledgements
[əkˈnɒlɪdʒmənts]

The following people were vital in the making of this book and the author wishes to thank them:

graphics design	André Luttermann	[ˌandʁeː ˈlʊtəman]
	www.tuerknacker.de	
proof-reading	Katja Fleming	[ˌkatjaː ˈflɛmɪŋ]
	Volker Lorenz	[ˌfɔlkɐ ˈloːʁɛnts]
	David Taylor	[ˌdeɪ̯vɪd ˈteɪlə]
	Stephanie Urban	[ˌstɛfəni ˈɜːbən]
	www.stephanie-urban.de	
proof-reading IPA	John Gledhill	[ˌdʒɒn ˈglɛdhɪl]
voice recording	Johnny Durham	[ˌdʒɒni ˈdʌrəm]
in the bigger picture	Beate Hampe	[beˌʔaːtə ˈhampə]